Transactions
of the
American Philosophical Society
Held at Philadelphia
For Promoting Useful Knowledge
Volume 89, Pt. 5

BENJAMIN FRANKLIN'S FIRST GOVERNMENT PRINTING:

The Pennsylvania General Loan Office Mortgage Register of 1729, and Subsequent Franklin Mortgage Registers and Bonds

KEITH ARBOUR

American Philosophical Society
Independence Square ❦ Philadelphia
1999

Copyright © 1999 by the American Philosophical Society for its *Transactions* series. All rights reserved.

ISBN:0-87169-895-1
US ISSN: 0065-9746

Library of Congress Cataloging-in-Publication Data

Arbour, Keith.
    Benjamin Franklin's first government printing : the Pennsylvania General Loan Office mortgage register of 1729 and subsequent Franklin mortgage registers and bonds / Keith Arbour.
    p.   cm. -- (Transactions of the American Philosophical Society, ISSN 0065-9746 ; v. 89, pt. 5)
Includes bibliographical references and index.
ISBN 0-87169-895-1 (paper)
    1. Franklin, Benjamin, 1706-1790. 2. Printing, Public--Pennsylvania--History-- 18th century. 3. Pennsylvania. General Loan Office. I. Title. II. Series.

Z232.F8 A73 1999
686.2'09748'09033--dc21
                                      99-052095

For

JANE & MALCOLM ARBOUR

extraordinary parents
awesome grandparents

CONTENTS

Acknowledgments vii
Location symbols ix
Discovery and Introduction 1
I. The 1729 Register and Subsequent Related Work in Context . . . 4
II. Evidence for the precise dating of the 1729 register and the first and second printed continuations of the 1726 register 34
III. Franklin and Meredith's, Franklin's, and Franklin and Hall's Mortgage Bond printing: Additions to Miller 40
Appendix: Index to mortgages recorded in the 1729 Pennsylvania General Loan Office Mortgage Register. 78
Index 88

ACKNOWLEDGMENTS

Too often rare historical artifacts are temporarily or permanently lost to scholarship when they are acquired by private collectors. (This can also occur when historical artifacts are acquired by public or semi-public institutions—but that is another story.) I hope that the history of the 1729 Pennsylvania General Loan Office mortgage register, detailed in the following pages, suggests the nature of the loss to Benjamin Franklin's biographers and historians of early American printing that private ownership of the 1729 register could have entailed. Happily, no sooner was the register discovered by Clarence Wolf, and acquired by Jay Snider, than Mr. Snider made it available for intensive study. Mr. Snider also provided a stipend that covered my expenses during work on the present essay. I thank him for these generous acts.

During July, 1997, Mr. Snider placed the 1729 Register on deposit at the Library of the American Philosophical Society. There I was able to examine the register daily amidst the Society's fine collections of Frankliniana and related printed and manuscript Philadelphia documents. I thank my friends Mr. Roy Goodman, Ms. Elizabeth Carroll-Horrocks, Ms. Marian Christ, Mr. Scott DeHaven, and Dr. Martin Levitt of the Philosophical Society's Library, and all their colleagues, for their assistance during that month. I thank them as well for their help and hospitality during my research visits to the Philosophical Society before and since. I also thank Mr. Frank Margeson for his photographs of Franklin mortgage bonds in the Philosophical Society's collections (see section III of the present study, nos. 8, 10, 11, and 14).

At the Bucks County Historical Society, Librarian Betsy Smith introduced me to the collections, and provided photographs of the only known survivors of Franklin's 1733 and 1734 editions of mortgage bonds for Pennsylvania's 1731 re-emission of paper money (section III, nos. 5 and 6). At the Historical Society of Delaware, Dr. Constance J. Cooper facilitated my searches through the Society's collection of small deeds, and provided photographs of the only known survivors of Franklin's 1729 and 1759 Delaware mortgage bonds (nos. 2 and 16). At the New Jersey State Archives, Trenton, reference librarian Bette Epstein and archivist Joseph Klett introduced me to the early printed and manuscript records of New Jersey counties, and facilitated the photographing of New Jersey's Bradford and Franklin printed mortgage registers (figs. C and D, and no. 7). I thank these curators for their assistance and for their expressions of interest in the present study.

At the Historical Society of Pennsylvania, the reading room staff provided prompt, professional, and courteous access to materials in their collections. I thank the Society for photographs of the unique Franklin mortgage bonds in its collections (nos. 3 and 4) and of an example of the manuscript indentures that preceded the Pennsylvania General Loan Office's resort to printed bonds (fig. B). At the City of Philadelphia, Department of Records, City Archives, Ms. Cindy Blichasz, Mr. Jefferson M. Moak, and Mr. Ward Child, City Archivist, provided friendly and efficient access to the city's early Loan Office registers—both before and after removal of the City Archives from Broad to Market streets. I thank them for this help, and for facilitating Mr. Will Brown's photographic visit to the Archives in their new location. I also thank Mr. Brown for the care with which he photographed these bonds (nos. 9, 12, 13, and 15), Bradford's 1724 New Jersey bond (figs. C and D), Franklin's 1737 New Jersey bonds (no. 7), and the Snider volume (fig. A, and no. 1).

Prof. Leo Lemay and Mr. James N. Green read this work in draft and provided helpful comments. Work on the Snider volume occasioned my introduction to Prof. C. William Miller, who made several helpful suggestions and challenged several of my points in draft and is thus responsible for what I hope are strengthenings of some of my arguments. I thank these old and new friends for their assistance. None of them is responsible for any errors or infelicities that may remain in the pages that follow, nor is Ms. Carole LeFaivre-Rochester, who copyedited the manuscript and saw the work through production, for which I thank her.

Lastly, I thank Clarence Wolf for asking me to confirm his thoughts on the 1729 register, for offering the register only to a collector certain to preserve the volume's integrity, and for introducing me to Jay Snider. And I thank Jay Snider again for lifting the bushel under which the 1729 register had been hidden for over 250 years. The dedication at the front of the present study speaks for itself; but to it I would add that this little monograph is also for

C. William Miller
on whose work we all depend

Keith Arbour

LOCATION SYMBOLS

CtY	Yale University
DeHi	Historical Society of Delaware
DLC	Library of Congress
FRLL	Friends Reference Library, London, England
MH-L	Harvard University Law School Library
Nj	New Jersey State Library (Archives)
NN	New York Public Library
PDoHi	Bucks County Historical Society
PHC	Haverford College
PHi	Historical Society of Pennsylvania
PPAmP	American Philosophical Society
PPL	Library Company of Philadelphia
PPRF	Rosenbach Foundation Library
PU	University of Pennsylvania
RPJCB	John Carter Brown Library

Fig. A. Front cover and spine of the 1729 Pennsylvania General Loan Office Mortgage Register, strengthened in 1996 by Fred Shihadeh. Courtesy Jay Snider.

DISCOVERY & INTRODUCTION

Among the items acquired in 1996 by Jay Snider, the collector of printed Americana, are 278 partially printed, early Pennsylvania mortgage forms. The royal folio forms (identical but for manuscript completions) are bound together, as issued, in full calf stamped with tools thought to have belonged to William Davies, a bookbinder who flourished in Philadelphia from 1722 to 1740 (fig. A).[1] The mortgage forms include printed preambles identifying Pennsylvania's General Loan Office trustees as the mortgagees, and manuscript completions dated as early as September 23, 1729. Clarence Wolf, the antiquarian book dealer who sold the volume to Mr. Snider, had previously purchased the volume from another book dealer because he recognized that it was probably printed by Andrew Bradford or Benjamin Franklin. Mr. Wolf knew that if Franklin had printed it, the volume could prove to be one of the earliest productions of the printing office Franklin and Hugh Meredith established in Philadelphia in 1728.

While cataloguing this volume, which was unknown to historians and bibliographers until Mr. Wolf called it to our attention and is therefore not in C. William Miller's descriptive bibliography *Benjamin Franklin's Philadelphia Printing, 1728-1766*, Mr. Wolf established that it was printed by Benjamin Franklin and Hugh Meredith with their first font of pica type.[2] He also noted that it was printed on imported sheets of paper (watermarked with a Strasburg bend and lily and countermarked IV) which Franklin and Meredith were known to have used in other jobs of the period.[3]

As soon as Mr. Snider acquired this previously unimagined artifact of Franklin and Meredith's earliest years in business, he made it available to historians for more extensive study. In the pages that follow I have

---

[1] The tools used on the Snider volume's binding are stamp a, roll 2, and (perhaps) double fillet A and triple fillet B, listed *sub* William Davies's name in C. William Miller, *Benjamin Franklin's Philadelphia Printing, 1728-1766*, Memoirs of the American Philosophical Society, vol. 102 (Philadelphia: American Philosophical Society, 1974), p. 522. The Snider binding is also stamped with an elaborate roll not recorded in Miller's Appendix C.

[2] See C. William Miller, "Benjamin Franklin's Philadelphia Type," *Studies in Bibliography*, XI (1958): 179-206.

[3] Cf. W. A. Churchill, *Watermarks in Paper in Holland, England, France, etc., in the XVII and XVIII Centuries and Their Interconnection* (Amsterdam: M. Hertzberger, 1935; repr. Nieuwkoop: De Graaf, 1990), plate CCCXXVII, no. 437. Miller calls this watermark simply "Strasbourg bend." Miller, *Benjamin Franklin's Philadelphia Printing*, no. 18.

attempted to place the Snider volume in its historical, political, biographical, and bibliographical contexts. The first section of the essay incorporates the volume's production into a narrative of Franklin and Meredith's first two years in business as independent printers. During these years the Pennsylvania Assembly's contest with lieutenant governor Patrick Gordon over the issue of paper money loomed large over the Pennsylvania economy—and over the lives of young tradesmen like Franklin and Meredith, whose success depended partly on a money supply sufficient for an expanding economy.

The first section also attempts to refine our chronology of Franklin and Meredith's earliest printing. In the process it establishes that the Snider volume was Benjamin Franklin's first officially commissioned job for any branch or agency of Pennsylvania's government. As such, the printing of this volume was probably the reward Franklin's friends in the Pennsylvania Assembly secured for him as thanks for publication of his pro-paper money pamphlet, *A Modest Inquiry into the Nature and Necessity of a Paper-Currency*. This discovery enables us to emend previous editors' annotations of the passage in the *Autobiography* in which Franklin stated that his Assembly friends rewarded him for his advocacy of paper money "by employing me in printing the Money, a very profitable Jobb"—but a job historians have long known was executed by Andrew Bradford, not Franklin and Meredith.[4]

Section II considers typographical and other evidence for the precise dating of the 1729 Pennsylvania General Loan Office Mortgage Register (the Snider volume), and Franklin and Meredith's two printed continuations of the Loan Office's 1726 manuscript register, neither of which is recorded in *Benjamin Franklin's Philadelphia Printing*. Although I have been able to establish relatively narrow ranges of dates for the printing of these three editions of mortgage forms, I have been no more successful than the editors of *Lawmaking & Legislators in Pennsylvania: A Biographical Dictionary* in discovering two related dates.[5] As mentioned in section II, we do not know the exact date of General Loan Office trustee Nathaniel Newlin's death, nor the exact date of Philip Taylor's appointment as Newlin's replacement. Perhaps calling attention here to these lost dates will further their discovery.

---

[4] Franklin, *Writings*, ed. by Lemay, 1368. For a representative annotation of this passage, see *The Autobiography of Benjamin Franklin*, ed. by Leonard W. Labaree, Ralph L. Ketcham, Helen C. Boatfield, and Helene H. Fineman (New Haven: Yale University Press, 1964), 124n4.

[5] Craig W. Horle, and others, *Lawmaking & Legislators in Pennsylvania: A Biographical Dictionary*, 2 vols. to date (Philadelphia: University of Pennsylvania Press, 1991-).

Discovery & Introduction

Section III comprises bibliographical descriptions of the 1729 General Loan Office Register, later Pennsylvania and New Jersey mortgage registers, and separate Pennsylvania and Delaware blank mortgage bonds printed by Franklin or his printing office through 1759. *Benjamin Franklin's Philadelphia Printing* was the first bibliography of a colonial American press to pay detailed attention to job printing (of handbills, posters, receipts, legal blanks like these mortgage forms, etc.) and its importance to the economic health of colonial North American printing offices.[6] This final section, which takes Prof. Miller's bibliography as its model, will, I hope, serve as an extension of his work.

Following section III is an Appendix that indexes all the mortgages recorded in the Snider volume.

---

[6] Georgia B. Barnhill summarizes some of C. William Miller's entries for Franklin and Meredith's, Franklin's, and Franklin and Hall's job printing in "Benjamin Franklin's Job Printing," *The Ephemera Journal* 8 (1998): 10-15.

I
THE 1729 REGISTER & SUBSEQUENT RELATED WORK IN CONTEXT

Throughout the following narrative I have emphasized: (1) Franklin's attempt to secure an appointment as printer to the Pennsylvania Assembly; (2) Pennsylvania's several paper money acts as causes of, and responses to, the business climate in which Franklin and Meredith worked from 1728 to 1730; (3) previously known Franklin and Meredith imprints produced during these years, with particular reference to aspects of Franklin's non-governmental work that compare unfavorably to printing for the government in general and work on the 1729 Register in particular; (4) the printing of the 1729 Register as a result of Franklin's aggressive response to his integrated analyses of the other three topics emphasized.

Late in May, 1728, Benjamin Franklin and Hugh Meredith (22 and about 31 years old, respectively) quit working for the Philadelphia printer Samuel Keimer, whom Franklin neither respected nor liked. Franklin and Meredith formed a business partnership and, with money Meredith's father advanced towards the purchase of a press and type, established a printing office of their own in a house they rented from Simon Edgell at what would now be 139 Market Street.[7] Only the central location (at which Franklin remained until the end of 1738) and Franklin's participation in the venture were propitious. Meredith, though often sober, had weaknesses for alcohol and gambling.

The new partnership had to compete with two established printers, Andrew Bradford and Keimer. William Bradford, who had brought printing to Philadelphia in 1685 and then to New York in 1693, had set his son Andrew up in Philadelphia in 1713. From then until 1723 the younger Bradford had built his business without local competition and with the cooperation of his father's New York office, which continued beyond that year. In 1728 young Bradford enjoyed regular traffic and the enviable boon of dependable printing orders from the provincial government, the first of which (for Evans 1644) he had successfully solicited during his first year in Philadelphia.[8] Outside of Boston, government business remained important to the maintenance of printing in the

---

[7] J.A. Leo Lemay, *Benjamin Franklin: A Documentary History*, © 1997. (www.english.udel.edu/lemay/franklin/), 1728: 1 June.

[8] Anna Janney DeArmond, *Andrew Bradford, Colonial Journalist* (Newark, Del.: University of Delaware Press, 1949), chap. 2.

few other American cities that had presses.⁹

Samuel Keimer had printed in Philadelphia since 1723. Franklin had worked for him twice, first during Keimer's start-up year, then in 1727-28.¹⁰ Franklin's assistance had helped Keimer stay afloat, perhaps despite himself, as had another lucky coincidence. Keimer had initially established his office just in time to profit from Pennsylvania's first emissions of paper money.¹¹ In 1723-24 these emissions released £45,000 in bills of credit into the Pennsylvania economy. This action reversed the local economic depression that had followed the implosion of the South Sea Company investment bubble in England in 1720.¹²

The first emission act of 1723 had established Pennsylvania's General Loan Office with a small board of trustees responsible for its affairs. The Loan Office's duty was to issue bills of credit to Pennsylvanians who mortgaged their real property to the Loan Office for an amount they received in newly created paper bills. The emission acts required Pennsylvanians to repay these loans over a set period of time, and the trustees to destroy ("sink" in the language of the times) the bills thus taken in repayment. While the bills remained in circulation, Pennsylvanians (like other colonists, chronically short of hard currency) temporarily enjoyed a standard medium of exchange, which improved commerce.

For the common good, each emission act should have permitted the money supply to increase as the Pennsylvania economy expanded. However, many wealthy residents of the province, and wealthier non-resident Penns, opposed this. They feared inflation, which hurts wealthier creditors as much as it helps poorer debtors.¹³ And so they attempted to

---

⁹ In Newport, Rhode Island, for instance, Benjamin Franklin's older brother and former master James Franklin found the transplantation of his printing office from Boston to Newport eased by the governmental commissions he began to receive regularly starting in June, 1728, during his second year in business there. See *Rhode Island Imprints, 1727-1800*, ed. by John Eliot Alden (New York: R.R. Bowker, for the Bibliographical Society of America, 1949), 5-7, (nos. 12 and 17), *et passim*.

¹⁰Franklin, *Writings*, ed. by Lemay, 1331, 1339, 1354-1356.

¹¹Pennsylvania, *The Statutes at Large of Pennsylvania from 1682 to 1801*, comp. by James T. Mitchell and Henry Flanders, vol. III, pp. 324-362, 389-407.

¹² The South Sea Company was a London-based joint-stock company. Its publicly traded shares commanded higher and higher prices from the company's inception in 1711 to its collapse in 1720 (when it became apparent that the stock prices had long since ceased to reflect either the company's assets or potential). So widespread had been the vogue for South Sea shares that their collapse shook England's economy and, with it, Anglo-American trade. John Carswell's *The South Sea Bubble* (Stanford, Cal.: Stanford Univ. Press, 1960) is the standard work on the subject, but see also John K. Galbraith, *A Short History of Financial Euphoria* (N.p.: Whittle Direct Books, 1990), despite its imprint.

¹³ Franklin, *Writings*, ed. by Lemay, p. 1367.

permit only emission acts that required relatively high rates of interest, relatively short loans, and the relatively prompt sinking of emissions. Sounder policy would have entailed a more flexible approach to the money supply. But until sound theory triumphed over the inconsiderateness of the wealthy, Pennsylvania would have to experience economic contractions before its farmers and tradesmen could pressure new acts through the Assembly.

The first act of 1723 directed the General Loan Office to emit £15,000 in printed bills of credit. The act limited the bills' currency to eight years and required that before eight years and five months had passed the trustees were to have sunk the entire emission.[14] This quickly proved insufficient to restart an economy depressed by the burst Bubble. The second 1723 emission act required the Loan Office to issue an additional £30,000 in bills of credit. But as the Loan Office took bills emitted under both acts in repayment and sunk them according to schedule, many Pennsylvanians noticed the check thereby placed on growth and requested further relief. In response, on March 5, 1726, the Assembly passed "An act for the re-emitting [on new mortgages] and continuing the currency of such bills of credit of this province as by former acts are directed to be sunk and destroyed, and for the striking and making current £10,000 in new bills, to supply those that are torn and defaced."[15]

When Franklin and Meredith left Keimer to establish their own printing office in the spring of 1728, Pennsylvania's economy was healthy as a result of this legislation. But it was growing at a pace that the predetermined money supply could not long sustain. Some residents of Philadelphia County had already petitioned the Assembly for a further emission.[16] During the following months more and more Pennsylvanians would notice that bills of credit were again becoming scarce.[17] As this scarcity increased it hindered business from growing as quickly as colonial immigration, productivity, and demand warranted.

There was, nonetheless, work to be had. Soon after setting up their own press, Franklin and Meredith benefitted from Samuel Keimer's inability to complete a large job. In 1725 Keimer had begun to reprint Samuel Sewel's *History of the Quakers* (a 700-page folio) for the Philadelphia Yearly Meeting. Keimer was not close to finishing this job when

---

[14] Pennsylvania, *Statutes at Large*, vol. III, p. 329.

[15] Pennsylvania, *Statutes at Large*, vol. IV, pp. 38-51.

[16] *Pennsylvania Archives*, ser. 8, vol. 3, p. 1867; cf. pp. 1869, 1871-74, 1876, 1879.

[17] *Pennsylvania Archives*, ser. 8, vol. 3, pp. 1914, 1917.

Franklin and Meredith quit working for him. The new partners knew that Keimer was unlikely to complete his edition of Sewel in a timely fashion without their help; yet they could hardly have returned to their old master to request work on Sewel. They therefore turned to the Yearly Meeting itself—unless while still working for Keimer they had already done this behind Keimer's back preparatory to setting up their own office.[18] In either case, Franklin's friend Joseph Breintnall was the young printers' intermediary with the Yearly Meeting. (Breintnall was a scrivener highly skilled in the manuscript production of legal documents. He was as devoted as Franklin to the earning of leisure for self-education; and had recently joined Franklin in founding the Junto, a reading and debating club of similarly interested young tradesmen.)

As Franklin recalled in his memoirs, Breintnall intervened with the Quakers and "procur'd us . . . the Printing [of] 40 [actually 44½] Sheets of their History, the rest being to be done by Keimer."[19] This was by far the largest job they handled during their first year in business: 500 copies of 44½ sheets (178 pages) [Miller 1; PHi, PPAmP, PPL, PU, et al]. According to Leo Lemay, they remained busy with their portion of the edition from July to October, 1728.[20] If Franklin was accurate in stating that he "compos'd of it a Sheet a Day, and Meredith work'd it off at Press,"[21] their work on it consumed about eight weeks of business days within this period.

Sometime after they finished work on Sewel, Franklin and Meredith printed Ralph Sandiford's anti-slavery tract, *A Brief Examination of the Practice of the Times* [Miller 11; CtY, PHi, PHC, PPL, PPRF; FRLL]. In the elliptical phrasing common to imprints of the period, this tract's title-page specifies the author, rather than the printers, as the risk-taking party in its manufacture, that is, as its publisher: "Printed for the Author, *Anno* 1729." This means that Franklin and Meredith undertook the printing of this work at the author's expense: Sandiford paid them for their materials and labor either up front or promptly upon completion of the job. The arrangement insured the partners a risk-free return on their investment in materials, time, and labor;[22] and the shy imprint enabled

---

[18] I think it highly likely that Franklin and Meredith left Keimer only after Franklin had arranged to pick up work on Sewel as soon as he and Meredith set up their own press, but have located no relevant documentary evidence.

[19] Franklin, *Writings*, ed. by Lemay, p. 1362.

[20] J.A. Leo Lemay, *Benjamin Franklin: A Documentary History*, 1728: note between 1 and 4 July.

[21] Franklin, *Writings*, ed. by Lemay, p. 1362.

[22] Cf. James N. Green's article on works Franklin published at his own risk, "Benjamin

Franklin and Meredith, still unsure of their suppers, to distance their business from Sandiford's impolitic, liberal discussion of his contemporaries' enslavement of African and African-American men, women, and children.

Sandiford dated his dedication of the work to Matthew Hughes, January 1, 1729. Franklin and Meredith probably set and printed the entire book within the month. A single copy of the book comprises twelve half-sheets in fours: 8vo, A-M^4. The number of copies in the edition is not known. But even if Sandiford ordered the printing of 500 copies, the job was less than one-seventh the size of their work on Keimer's edition of Sewel. It was nonetheless welcome work. Riskless opportunities proposed by individual authors did not enter new printers' offices every day. Nor could young printers like Franklin count on them in business forecasts.

Government printing, on the other hand, also entailed riskless profit. Moreover, once a good colonial printer had secured one government commission, he or she could reasonably count on additional, predictably periodic commissions. Knowing this, Franklin drafted a hopeful petition to the Pennsylvania Assembly in February 1729. He requested that he and Meredith be hired to execute some of the provincial government's official printing. The petition has not been located; but in it Franklin probably recommended the partnership's ability to print the next volume of the Pennsylvania Assembly's *Journal*. He may have implied or asserted that he and Meredith could print it in a more elegant style than the Assembly was used to seeing, for less money than it was accustomed to paying.

On February 18, the clerk of the Pennsylvania Assembly recorded that "The petition of Hugh Meredith, and Benjamin Franklin, praying to print for the province, was read, and ordered to lie of the table."[23] The Assembly records include no further mention of the petition. As Leo Lemay has noted, Franklin and Meredith "did not have enough support to bring their request to a vote." Politicians cannot be turned so easily. Four days later the House "Ordered, that Andrew Bradford print the said minutes [i.e. Evans 3200]."[24] So Bradford kept his hold on government printing for the nonce.

"About this Time," Franklin recalled when writing his memoirs, "there was a Cry among the People for more Paper-Money, only 15,000£

Franklin as Bookseller and Publisher," pp. 98-114 in *Reappraising Franklin: A Bicentennial Perspective*, ed. by J.A. Leo Lemay (Newark: University of Delaware Press, 1993).

[23] *Pennsylvania Archives*, series 8, vol. 3, p. 1928.

[24] J.A. Leo Lemay, *Benjamin Franklin: A Documentary History*, 1729: 22 February.

being extant in the Province & that soon to be sunk."²⁵ Even as Franklin launched his partnership's attempt to gain Assembly business, the Assembly was finalizing a new money bill that responded to these Pennsylvanians' complaints. Franklin was as interested in the government's response to the clamor for more money as he was in its response to his direct request for government business. He knew that any significant increase in the money supply would improve his and Meredith's business prospects—along with those of most other clever and energetic Philadelphia workers. A failure to increase the money supply, on the other hand, would inevitably constrict Franklin and Meredith's business regardless of their industry and ingenuity.

On the same day that the Assembly tabled Franklin and Meredith's printing petition, it directed several chosen members to carry a liberal money bill to Governor Patrick Gordon for his approval. (The Assembly also directed its messengers to take with them a £500 check "payable to the Governor towards Support of Government.")²⁶ Gordon recognized the need for more bills of credit, but was also loyal to his employers, the wealthy, non-resident Penns. On March 25, 1729, he asked the Assembly to diminish the amount and duration of the proposed emission and increase the interest rate.²⁷ This exchange prompted further debate over the details of the next emission act. The debate would continue in the House and in Philadelphia houses and taverns through the first week of May, when the Assembly would vote out a bill that Governor Gordon would consent to sign.

In the meantime Franklin, deeply interested in the debate and its results, either read essays on economics that he had not read before, or reviewed economic writings that he had previously studied. He did this with an eye set on selecting thoughts, phrases, and passages relevant to the paper money debate. "I was on the Side of an Addition," Franklin later wrote, "being persuaded that the first small Sum struck in 1723 had done much good, by increasing the Trade, Employment, & Number of Inhabitants in the Province, since I now saw all the old Houses inhabited, & many new ones building, where as I remember'd well, that when I first walk'd about the Streets of Philadelphia, eating my Roll, I saw most of the Houses in Walnut street between Second & Front streets with Bills

---

[25] Franklin, *Writings*, ed. by Lemay, p. 1367.

[26] *Pennsylvania Archives*, ser. 8, vol. 3, p. 1928.

[27] *Colonial Records*, vol. 3, pp. 346-347. Gordon's message is printed in *Pennsylvania Archives*, ser. 8, vol. 3, pp. 1933-1936.

on their Doors, to be let."[28]

In or around early March, 1729 (or possibly much earlier), Franklin proposed paper money, its advantages and disadvantages, as a topic for his fellow tradesmen to discuss during a Junto meeting. At a subsequent meeting he or a friend presented an argument on the topic, and listened to one of their friends present a counter argument. All members attended to the resultant discussion. Franklin probably took particular care to note whichever statements pro and con seemed to carry the most weight with his fellow Junto members. Having thus gained a sense of the kind of arguments necessary to garner wide support for a generous emission act, he wrote an essay favoring an increase in paper money.[29]

But before Franklin transformed his manuscript essay into typepages, he seized an opportunity to demonstrate graphically the qualitative difference between his own office's printing and Andrew Bradford's. At the end of March the Assembly had Bradford print one of their periodic addresses to the governor. On or about March 29 or 30, Franklin saw the broadside [Evans 3203] and judged it printed "in a coarse blundering manner."[30] So he promptly "reprinted it elegantly & correctly, and sent one to every Member" of the Assembly gratis [Miller 9; no copy extant]. More than forty years later Franklin recalled the representatives' reactions: "They were sensible of the Difference, [and] it strengthen'd the Hands of our Friends in the House" as they worked to designate the young partners printers to the Assembly.[31]

Bradford's broadside printing of the Assembly's address is unlikely to have struck any of its first readers as having been printed "in a coarse blundering manner" until Franklin intimated as much while passing out his reprint. Leo Lemay has noted that "the type itself was worn-out and broken, so that many whole letters and numerous parts of letters did not quite print."[32] This accurate assessment is based on examination of the

---

[28] Franklin, *Writings*, ed. by Lemay, pp. 1367-1368.

[29] Franklin, *Writings*, ed. by Lemay, pp. 1367-1368. Francis Rawle (1660-1727) of Philadelphia wrote and published a similarly pro-money pamphlet a year after the South Sea bubble burst. He intended thereby to bring on the paper money act that was eventually passed in 1723. See his *Some Remedies Proposed, for the Restoring the Sunk Credit of the Province of Pennsylvania... Humbly Offer'd to the Consideration of the Worthy Representatives in the General Assembly of this Province* ([Philadelphia:] Printed [by Andrew Bradford] in the year, 1721) [Evans 2287; PPL, RPJCB].

[30] Franklin, *Writings*, ed. by Lemay, p. 1365.

[31] Franklin, *Writings*, ed. by Lemay, p. 1365.

[32] During final reading of the ms. of the present study, it was sensibly suggested that Evans 3203 may be Bradford's "fine broadside" reprinting of his own coarse *American Weekly Mercury* printing of the Assembly's address (personal communication). While I concur

sole extant exemplar. Differently inked exemplars may have looked slightly better—or slightly worse. Aside from its imperfect type and inking, however, the worst that could be urged against Bradford's broadside today is that its caption title is puny rather than grand—that it did not look much like its more elegant London or Boston counterparts.

No exemplar of Franklin and Meredith's edition survives for comparison. But Bradford's next official broadsides—the lieutenant governor's March 31, 1729, proclamation regarding good public order [Evans 3201] and his speech of April 2, 1729 [Evans 3202]—are extant. Typographically they are impressive responses to Franklin's criticism: at the head of both are elaborate, ornamented caption titles, which probably vied with that on Franklin's sophisticated reprinting of the previous address; and at the bottom of both are Bradford's explicit imprints (absent from Evans 3203) set in roman and italic type and including the epithet "Printer to the Province."[33] Large type, it seems, could be used even then to touch the vanity of politicians. Bradford immediately caught on; but the credit for what some Assemblymen considered that week's aesthetic improvement in official broadsides went to Franklin.

Franklin and Meredith's reprinting of the Assembly's March 29 address to Governor Gordon was a day's work. Franklin probably had it printed off, dried, and distributed before the end of the day following the publication of Bradford's edition. Then he returned to his pro-paper money essay, which he entitled *A Modest Enquiry into the Nature and Necessity of a Paper-Currency*. He finished polishing his composition on April 3, 1729; and he and Meredith finished printing it [Miller 4; PHi, PPL] and stitching it into paper covers sometime before April 10. On that day Andrew Bradford's newspaper *The American Weekly Mercury* carried a paid advertisement announcing that *A Modest Enquiry* had just

---

that Bradford's newspaper printing is textually inferior to the broadside printing (misprinting the salutation in the governor's response as "Gentlmen," and "Courts of Quarter-Sessions" as "Court of Quarter-Sessions"), I do not concur that it ante-dates the broadside. Nor do I think that if Franklin had responded to Bradford's newspaper printing with a fine broadside set in his new type, Bradford would have been inattentive (or foolish) enough to print another broadside edition set in inferior type. The sequence is more likely to have been this: (1) Bradford printed Evans 3203; (2) Franklin printed a finer broadside edition (now lost) of the same text; (3) Bradford reprinted the Assembly's address and the governor's response in the next issue of the *American Weekly Mercury*; and (4) Bradford took care to set his *next* official broadside (Evans 3201) as grandly, and print it as well, as Franklin had probably set and printed his reprinting of Bradford's Evans 3203.

[33] Cf. Franklin's broadside edition of Gov. Gordon's speech of January 13, 1729/30 [Miller 29; PHi].

been published.[34]

However small (within reason) Franklin and Meredith's edition of *A Modest Enquiry*, this was a larger job than the Assembly speech. But it was probably less than one-tenth the size of their job for Keimer. Franklin's manuscript translated into 4½ printed half-sheets in fours (8vo: A-D⁴ E²; 34 small pages of text, preceded by a title-leaf with blank verso). If they printed 600 copies (a likely figure, but only an estimate), the entire edition consumed around 1350 sheets—about as many as they had printed to produce thirty copies of their portion of Keimer's Sewel.

The pamphlet sold for sixpence, or $1\frac{1}{3}$d per perfected[35] half-sheet (the inexact equivalent of $2\frac{2}{3}$ d per perfected sheet—a figure we will later use as a basis for comparisons).[36] Given the extent of local interest in its topic and the timeliness of its publication, *A Modest Enquiry* probably generated a profit on sales. But though part of the edition sold briskly, the entire edition did not soon sell out. Prof. Miller has reported that more than two years after the partners printed it, Franklin "sent a dozen copies of the remainder to his brother James in Newport."[37] Money from the publication thus dripped in slowly, and unsurely—as was usual for such publications in colonial America. (If every reader of a pamphlet paid for it, printers' profits would have been greater. But the purchasers of most pamphlets shared them with other readers.) However, the lasting benefit Franklin gained from this work was greater than a balance sheet summary of its publication could show.

In April or May,[38] 1729, Franklin and Meredith printed the first American edition of Isaac Watts's translation of *The Psalms of David*

---

[34] *American Weekly Mercury*, April 3-10, 1729, p. 4, col. 2.

[35] Perfected: printed on both sides.

[36] Cf. Franklin's 1734 printing of *The Constitutions of the Free-Masons* [Miller 80], a small 4to of 12 sheets (A-M⁴), which he sold for 2s/6d, or $2\frac{1}{2}$d per perfected sheet.

[37] Miller, *Benjamin Franklin's Philadelphia Printing*, p. 4.

[38] This approximate dating is by no means certain. The earliest reference to this edition of the *Psalms* located by Prof. Miller is Franklin and Meredith's advertisement in their first issue of *The Pennsylvania Gazette* (October 2, 1729), where they described the *Psalms* as "lately printed," rather than "just printed." Had the partners printed the *Psalms* as late as July or August, their October advertisement would probably read "Just printed." This suggests that this edition was already at least several months old—and perhaps older—by October 2, 1729. In June 1731 Franklin referred to this edition of the *Psalms* when he wrote, "I have known a very numerous Impression of *Robin Hood's Songs* go off in this Province at 2 s. per Book, in less than a Twelvemonth; when a small Quantity of *David's Psalms* (an excellent Version) have lain upon my Hands above twice the Time" (Franklin, *Writings*, ed. by Lemay, p. 173). Counting "above twice" twelve months back from June, 1731, takes us to some unspecified month before June 1729.

[Miller 2; PHi]. Thomas Godfrey (1704-1749), Franklin's ingenious and difficult tenant, quixotically financed this edition in whole or part; and his name therefore appears in the imprint as publisher.[39] Only one copy of this edition survives; and no manuscript purchase inscription or other marginalia in it assists us in dating its production. Given the particular need for textual accuracy and typographical elegance in sacred texts, it is unlikely that the partners ran the twelve-and-a-half sheets of this work through the press in as many days. Rather, they are likely to have spent a month of work-days on it, allowing for intermittent attention to job printing requiring fractional days.

On May 10, 1729, about four weeks after Franklin published his pro-emission *Enquiry*, Governor Gordon approved "An Act for Emitting of Thirty Thousand Pounds in Bills of Credit for the Better Support of Government and the Trade of this Province."[40] Writing forty-two years after the event, Franklin recalled a connection between his pamphlet and approval of the act:

> I wrote and printed an anonymous Pamphlet on it, entituled, *The Nature and Necessity of a Paper Currency*. It was well receiv'd by the common People in general; but the Rich Men dislik'd it; for it increas'd and strengthen'd the Clamour for more Money; and they happening to have no Writers among them that were able to answer it, their Opposition slack'd, and the Point was carried by a Majority in the House. My Friends there, who conceiv'd I had been of some Service, thought fit to reward me, by employing me in printing the Money, a very profitable Jobb, and a great Help to me.[41]

Commenting on the last sentence, Franklin's editors have long asserted that his memory here played him false, that his friends in the

---

[39] J.A. Leo Lemay suspects that Godfrey did not finance this edition and that its imprint is some sort of "private joke" (Lemay, *Benjamin Franklin: A Documentary History*, © 1997 (www.english.udel.edu/lemay/franklin/), 1729: § Business). I suspect, rather, that Franklin asked the sometimes difficult Godfrey (with whom Franklin was perforce living) to help him by sharing in the risk and that Godfrey actually did so. Franklin knew that one way to smooth the path of friendship was to ask a favor likely to be granted. Cf. Franklin *Writings*, ed. by Lemay, p. 1403. For the best recent sketch of Godfrey see Whitfield J. Bell, Jr., *Patriot-Improvers: Biographical Sketches of Members of the American Philosophical Society*, 3 vols. (Philadelphia: APS, 1997-), vol. 1, pp. 62-67, where a typographical error on p. 63 gives 1727, rather than 1729, as the year Godfrey "commissioned Franklin and his partner Hugh Meredith to print an edition of Isaac Watts' *Psalms of David*."

[40] Pennsylvania, *Statutes at Large*, vol. IV, pp. 98-116.

[41] Franklin, *Writings*, ed. by Lemay, p. 1368.

Assembly did not immediately reward him with a printing job.[42] Indeed, we know that Andrew Bradford—not Franklin—printed the paper money emitted under the 1729 act and that Franklin was not awarded a Pennsylvania currency printing contract until 1731.[43] Nor is there any record of the Pennsylvania Assembly voting to have Franklin and Meredith print any other government documents before January 30, 1730.[44]

The newly discovered Snider volume of mortgage bonds, however, suggests that Franklin's memory did not play him as false as we have long thought. With the Snider volume as evidence, we can now evaluate more fully than was previously possible the accuracy of Franklin's account of this incident. But before we turn to this volume for the details it adds to our reconstruction of Franklin and Meredith's first year in business and how they became the Assembly's printers, it will be worthwhile to return briefly to the early Pennsylvania currency acts. Their provisions for the printing of money and the keeping of General Loan Office records are also important to this reconstruction.

From the first, Pennsylvania's several emission acts required the printing of the bills of credit that constituted every emission.[45] The printing of these bills was carried out under constant official surveillance that occasionally must have seemed awkward for tradesmen as independent-minded as printers often were. The type, ornaments, and wood- or metal-cuts for money printed by the relief process had to be kept under lock and key when not in use. The number of sheets pulled had to be counted carefully every day and recounted at several subsequent stages and the counts had to tally. In short, contrary to regular printing-house practices, nothing could be left simply hanging about.

The acts also required that several specially designated men who were not Loan Office trustees sign and number each and every bill by hand, with pen and ink.[46] After these operations, the entire emission was

---

[42] See, e.g. *The Autobiography of Benjamin Franklin*, ed. by Leonard W. Labaree and others (New Haven: Yale University Press, 1964), p. 124 n. 4. Cf. Esmond Wright, *Franklin of Philadelphia* (Cambridge: Harvard University Press, 1986), p. 37.

[43] Eric P. Newman, *The Early Paper Money of America* (Racine, Wisc.: Whitman Publishing Co., 1967), pp. 237-238.

[44] On January 30, 1730, the House voted that Franklin and Meredith print "the Minutes of this House," i.e. *The Votes and Proceedings* of 1729-30. Franklin and Meredith published the first part of this volume in May, 1730, and the second in August, 1730 [Miller 28]. See also J.A. Leo Lemay, *Benjamin Franklin: A Documentary History*, 1729: § "Business"; and 1730: § "Business."

[45] Pennsylvania, *Statutes at Large*, vol. III, p. 324.

[46] Pennsylvania, *Statutes at Large*, vol. III, p. 325.

transferred to the Loan Office trustees, who counted the bills all over again upon receipt. The sheets of signed, hand-numbered bills were then cut up into the small pieces of paper that actually circulated through the province.[47] (The money may not have been cut until the Loan Office trustees were disbursing it.) All of these operations intervened between the passage of money acts and the actual emission of the paper bills.

The printing and readying of money for public circulation was thus a time-consuming and in some ways grave process, far from the casual printing of a broadside poem or yet another slim pamphlet. All men involved in the work had to be trusted members of the community, known quantities with solid credit, sound reputations, and allies among Pennsylvania's ruling groups. Andrew Bradford was chosen to print the province's paper money in 1723 and 1726.[48] In the spring or summer of 1729 he was chosen to print it once again—just as he had been chosen on February 22 to print the Assembly's *Votes*, notwithstanding Franklin and Meredith's petition.

So Bradford printed the £30,000 in bills of credit authorized by the act for which Franklin had energetically lobbied. (As Franklin had foreseen, passage of the act benefitted all Pennsylvanians.) The province paid Bradford £80 for the job.[49] This large sum confirms how great a trust the printing of the money was. It also indicates that the job monopolized Bradford's printing office for an appreciable part of the summer.[50] Indeed, so great was the job that in the spring of 1729 Franklin ought perhaps to have known—and may have sensed—that it was too important for the province to entrust to an officially untested pair of young printers, one of whom drank. But how Franklin yearned to be hired!

In addition to requiring the printing of money, the first 1723 emission act had also required that Loan Office trustees "or some of them, shall, at their own proper costs and charges, provide good large books of royal or other large paper, and well covered [i.e. bound],

---

[47] For a fine reproduction of a signed but uncut sheet of a later issue of Pennsyvlania paper currency, see E. McSherry Fowble, *Two Centuries of Prints in America, 1680-1880: A Selective Catalogue of the Winterthur Museum Collection* (Charlottesville: Univ. Press of Virginia, for The Henry Francis du Pont Winterthur Museum, 1987), pp. 510-11 (cat. no. 371), and color plate preceding p. 1.

[48] Newman, *The Early Paper Money of America*, pp. 236-237.

[49] *Pennsylvania Archives*, series 8, vol. 3, p. 2043.

[50] When Samuel Keimer, with Franklin as his journeyman, printed New Jersey paper money at Burlington in 1728, they appear to have spent about two months on the job. Lemay, *Benjamin Franklin: A Documentary History*, 1728: § "Personal." On this trip to Burlington Franklin may well have seen one of the printed mortgage registers that Andrew Bradford had printed for each New Jersey county in 1724.

wherein shall be recorded and enrolled all the deeds of mortgages to be taken for bills of credit to be let out upon loan, according to the directions of this act, in a fair, legible hand."[51] Subsequent acts reiterated this requirement in nearly identical terms, although the clause "in a fair, legible hand" was not repeated in the 1726 act.[52]

Loan Office trustees satisfied the requirements of the 1723 and 1726 laws by procuring bound royal folio volumes of wholly blank paper for the recording in manuscript of all mortgages granted under these laws. From 1723 to 1729 Loan Office clerks enrolled the mortgages in good copybook handwriting one after another (painstakingly repeating all the formulaic legal phrases) on the rectos and versos of these royal folio leaves (fig. B).[53] They did this after they had formally engrossed the original mortgages on separate sheets of paper, which had then been signed by the principals, sealed, witnessed, and notarized. (Each enrolled copy exactly duplicated the original mortgage—including all dates appearing on it, even though the scrivener may have enrolled the mortgage one or more days after its notarization date.)

The 1729 act followed the precedents of 1723 and 1726 by requiring that the Loan Office trustees "shall at their own proper costs and charges provide [the] said books of [royal] or [other] large, good paper, well bound and covered, wherein shall be recorded all the said deeds of mortgage given in security for the said bills of credit to be lent out as aforesaid."[54] The trustees could have satisfied this stipulation by procuring another volume of wholly blank paper, just as they always had. Nothing in the law suggested they do otherwise.

Yet back in 1726 Andrew Bradford might well have suggested they do otherwise. In 1724 he had printed hundreds of blank mortgage forms (folio broadsheets with un-printed versos) for the recording of mortgages executed in New Jersey under that province's 1723 act for the emission of £40,000 in paper money (fig. C).[55] Because Bradford profited from his printings of these blank forms, it is unlikely that he would have neglected to suggest the printing of similar forms to Pennsylvania's Loan Office

---

[51] Pennsylvania, *Statutes at Large*, vol. III, p. 327.

[52] Pennsylvania, *Statutes at Large*, vol. III, p. 397; vol. IV, p. 42.

[53] The first manuscript register is extant. Historical Society of Pennsylvania, MS Collection no. 902 (Am|.266|vol. 2). See fig. B.

[54] Pennsylvania, *Statutes at Large*, vol. IV, p. 107.

[55] In 1955 C. William Miller identified two partly printed Burlington County, New Jersey, Loan Office registers in the New Jersey Archives, Trenton, as the work of Andrew Bradford. In the first are enrolled mortgages dated April 1724 to May 1733; in the second, the mortgages are dated April 1733 to April 1746. See Miller, "Franklin's Type: Its Study Past and Present," *Proceedings of the American Philosophical Society*, 99 (1955): 418-432, esp. p. 425.

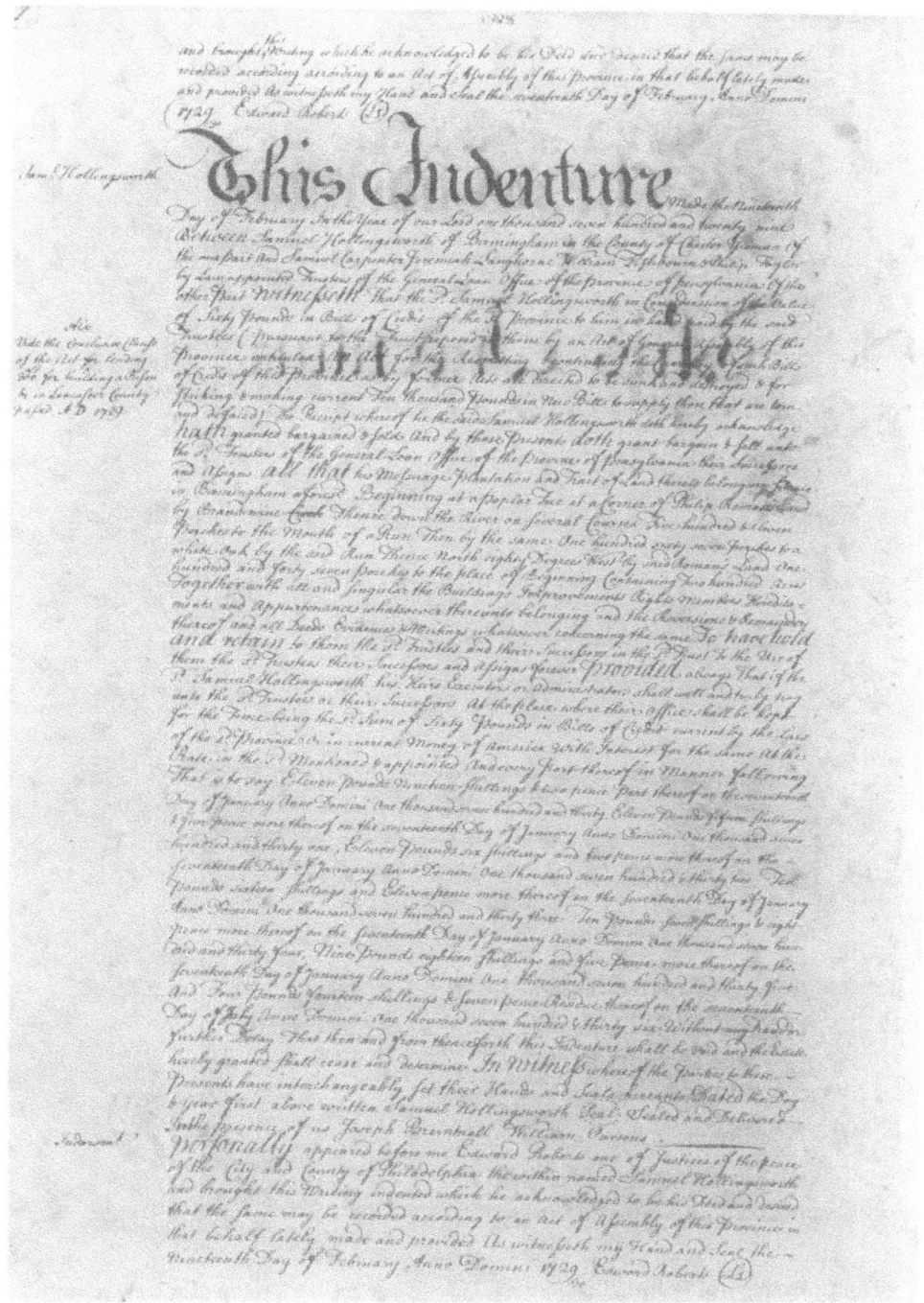

Fig. B. Wholly manuscript mortgage, page 328, from the 1726 Pennsylvania General Loan Office Mortgage Register. Courtesy the Historical Society of Pennsylvania.

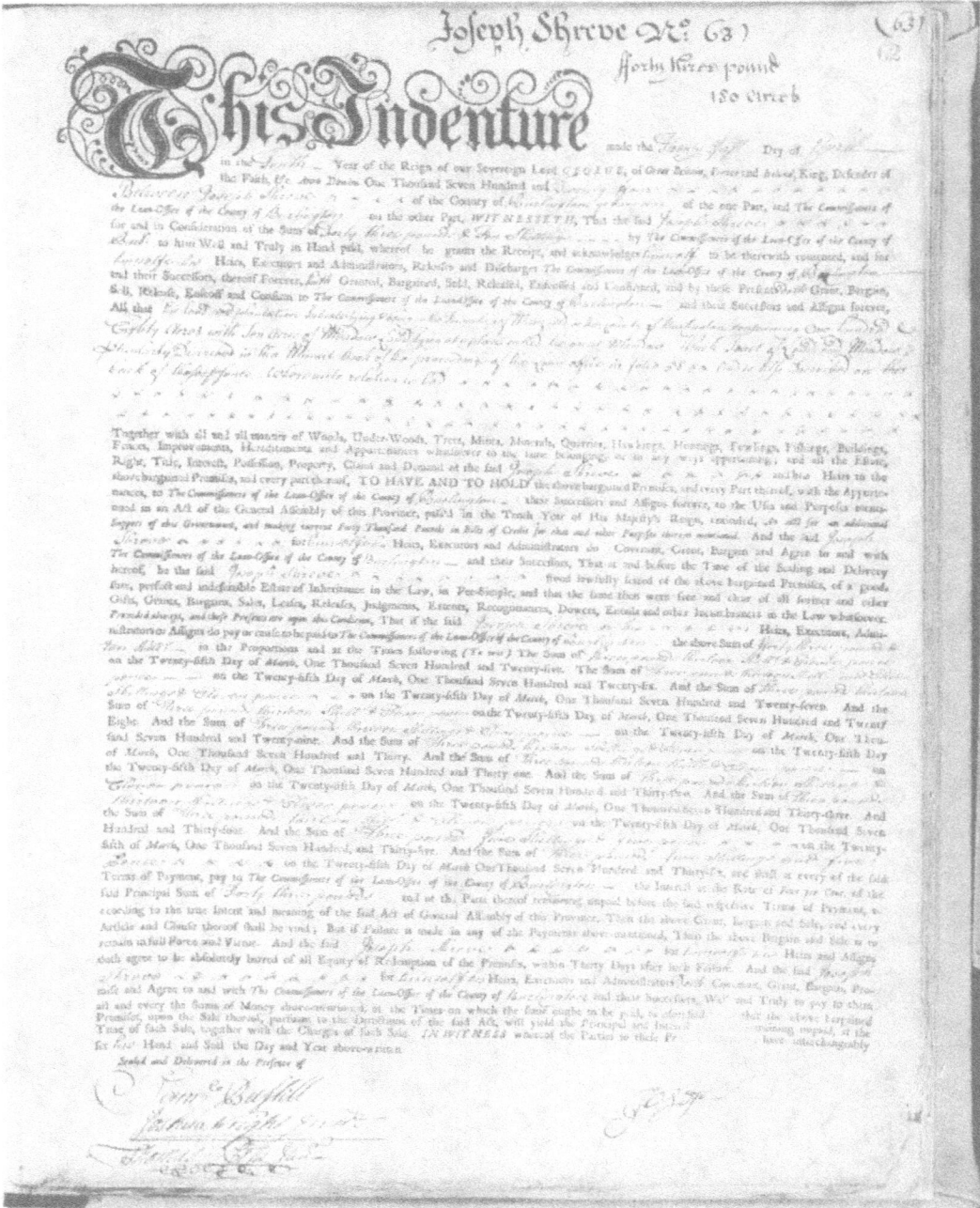

Fig. C. Example of William Bradford's 1724 mortgage register printing for New Jersey counties: leaf 63 from the Burlington County Loan Office Mortgage Register. Courtesy New Jersey State Archives.

The 1729 Register &c. in Context

ies, Hawkings, Huntings, Fowlings, Fishings, Buildings,
ing, or in any ways appertaining; and all the Estate,
eve *&* *&* *&* *&* *&* *&* and his Heirs to the
argained Premises, and every Part thereof, with the Appurte-
ors and Assigns forever, to the Uses and Purposes menti-
His Majesty's Reign, entituled, *An Act for an additional
other Purposes therein mentioned.* And the said *Joseph*
do Covenant, Grant, Bargain and Agree to and with
hat at and before the Time of the Sealing and Delivery
wfully seized of the above bargained Premises, of a good,
same then were free and clear of all former and other
rs, Entails and other Incumbrances in the Law whatsoever.

Fig. D. Detail from figure C, showing the quality of Bradford's inking. Courtesy New Jersey State Archives.

ights, Members, Hereditaments, and Appurtenances whatsoever
of, and all Deeds, Evidences and Writings whatsoever concern-
them the said Trustees and their Successors in the said Trust, to
ever, *PROVIDED always,* That if the said *Thomas*
hall well and truly pay unto the said Trustees or their Successors
;, the said Sum of *Thirty six Pounds*
Province, or in current Money of *America,* with Interest for the
very Part thereof; in manner following, That is to say *Four*
part thereof on the Fifteenth Day of *October, Anno Domini* One
ighteen shillings and nine pence more thereof
Seven Hundred and Thirty one; *Three pounds sixteen*
the Fifteenth Day of *October, Anno Domini* One Thousand Seven
lings, three pence more thereof on the

Fig. E. Detail of page 1 of Franklin and Meredith's 1729 Loan Office Mortgage Register, showing the quality of Franklin and Meredith's inking. Courtesy Jay Snider.

trustees. But the Pennsylvania trustees had not adopted this Bradford-New Jersey practice in 1726. Why?

Perhaps Charles Brockden, the eminent Philadelphia scrivener appointed clerk of the Loan Office under section XIV of the 1726 emission act, favored the continued engrossing and recording of mortgages wholly in manuscript.[56] Perhaps Brockden feared that the use of printed forms would entail a decrease in work for the clerks in his office and thus in his own income.[57] Perhaps one or more of the trustees thought the "fair, legible hand" clause of Pennsylvania's 1723 emission act remained an implied restriction on Loan Office record-keeping. Perhaps Bradford's New Jersey bonds struck someone in the Pennsylvania Loan Office as insufficiently neat: certainly some of the extant New Jersey forms are sloppily inked (fig. D).[58] Or perhaps the weight of custom or inertia decided the issue. These possibilities, however, are mere speculation. At this writing we know (or think we know) only that the Pennsylvania General Loan Office trustees did not have Andrew Bradford print a mortgage register for them in 1726.

Nor did the trustees have Bradford print a register for them in 1729. That year, however, the trustees did procure a printed register with text freshly adapted to the 1729 emission act. The register is now known to be extant. Comparison of the carefully inked letters impressed on its pages (fig. E) with all of the fonts employed by Philadelphia printers ca. 1729[59] proves that Franklin and Meredith printed it. Was this, then, the printing order with which Franklin's friends rewarded him for his effective advocacy of the 1729 emission act?

We know that the printing of the money itself was not Franklin's reward, despite his written statement to the contrary. We also know that his printing of Delaware paper money, which he undertook late in the fall of 1729, was not the reward. When writing his memoirs in 1771 Franklin correctly remembered that he had printed the Delaware money after he had profited from his Pennsylvania reward: "I soon *after* obtain'd, thro' my Friend Hamilton, the Printing of the NewCastle Paper Money, *another* profitable Jobb, as I then thought it; small Things

---

[56] Pennsylvania, *Statutes at Large*, vol. IV, p. 50.

[57] As far back as 1723-24 Franklin had been friends with some of the clerks in Charles Brockden's office. Franklin, *Writings*, ed. by Lemay, p. 1340.

[58] Burlington County, New Jersey, Loan Office register, 1724-1733. See, e.g., the leaf numbered "63" in manuscript (ink-stamped "64"), illustrated here as figs. C and D. New Jersey State Archives, Trenton.

[59] As catalogued by Prof. Miller in 1958. See Miller, "Benjamin Franklin's Philadelphia Type," *Studies in Bibliography*, 11 (1958): 179-206.

appearing great to those in small Circumstances" (emphasis added).[60]

Even though Franklin did not write of the 1729 Loan Office register as his reward for having supported the emission act, did he describe the reward in terms accurately transferable to (from) the register; that is, was the register as closely connected with the emission act as the money itself was, and therefore part and parcel of the same exchange of favors (unlike the Delaware money)? Were Franklin's friends connected with the order to print the register? Was its printing "a very profitable Jobb"? And was being awarded that job "a great Help" to Franklin?[61] In other words, when Franklin wrote of the events of 1729 forty-two years later, was it his actual printing of the register that he replaced with his fanciful printing of the money?

First, was the register as closely connected with the emission act as the money itself was? It was: Franklin and Meredith printed the register, as Bradford printed the money, for the General Loan Office in accordance with the 1729 emission act.

Second, were Franklin's friends in the House—who "conceived [he] had been of some Service, [and] thought fit to reward [him]"—able to designate the printer of the register, as they chose the printer of the money? They were. By passing the 1729 emission act, Franklin's House friends placed the Loan Office trustees in their debt for the continuation and augmentation of their large salaries.[62] In return for these salaries, the 1729 emission act required the trustees' investments of time, careful stewardship,[63] and the purchase of a folio mortgage register.[64] The difference between the prices of the customary bound folio of entirely blank pages (about £1, or 5s from each trustee)[65] and a bound folio of

---

[60] Franklin, *Writings*, ed. by Lemay, p. 1368.

[61] Franklin, *Writings*, ed. by Lemay, p. 1368.

[62] Pennsylvania, *Statutes at Large*, vol. IV, p. 102.

[63] The act required careful stewardship, but did not elicit it from all trustees. William Fishbourn was the first of two embezzling trustees whose crimes were uncovered during Franklin's lifetime. The other was John Kinsey. See Craig W. Horle, "William Fishbourne," in Craig W. Horle, and others, *Lawmaking & Legislators in Pennsylvania: A Biographical Dictionary*, 2 vols. to date (Philadelphia: University of Pennsylvania Press, 1991-), vol. 2, pp. 366-373; Edwin B. Bronner, "The Disgrace of John Kinsey, Quaker Politician, 1739-1750," *Pennsylvania Magazine of History and Biography* 75 (1951): 400-415; and Jeffrey L. Scheib, "John Kinsey," in Craig W. Horle, and others, *Lawmaking & Legislators in Pennsylvania*, vol. 2, pp. 591-606.

[64] Pennsylvania, *Statutes at Large*, vol. IV, p. 107. The trustees also had to post bond (p. 102).

[65] On June 22, 1731, Franklin charged Samuel Bustill £1/4s for a blank book comprising five quires of "large paper." The 1729 register comprises about three quires.

printed forms (approximately £2/4 to £2/13, or between 11s and 13s/3d from each trustee) represented to the trustees a small return favor easily directed to the designated object of some assemblymen's regard: Franklin and Meredith.

Third, was the printing of the Loan Office register "a very profitable Jobb"? The phrase derives much of its import from its context: Franklin's first years as master of his own printing office. As he recalled in his memoirs, even during his second year in business he thought some jobs very profitable that he later would have considered less so, "small Things appearing great to those in small Circumstances." And yet, though profits on editions of blank legal forms may have been "small Things appearing great to those in small Circumstances," they were neither as small, nor as uncertain as per-sheet profits on other jobs the partners executed during those years, like Franklin's own *Modest Enquiry*.

We have already noted that Franklin sold his pro-money pamphlet for 6d, or $1^1/_3$d per perfected half-sheet. This translates—roughly, but adequately for rudimentary comparison—into $2^2/_3$d per perfected sheet, retail. To estimate their profit per perfected sheet Franklin would have deducted estimated production expenses from the retail unit price. From $2^2/_3$d he therefore needed to deduct the cost of the sheet and the labor for four operations: setting into type continuous prose sufficient to cover both sides of the sheet, printing both sides of the sheet, folding the sheet, and stitching it to other sheets.[66]

We do not know how much Franklin charged for the 1729 register. For an entirely blank book of three quires of royal paper (24 sheets per quire) he would have charged about £1, of which five shillings went directly to its binder. If Franklin calculated the price of the register by adding to this figure (which includes, of course, the charge for the paper) a penny for the printing of each of the 288 bonds in the register (half of his wholesale price for bonds purchased in large quantities; adding the entire wholesale price would include a redundant charge for paper), he would have charged £2/4 for the whole job. If, on the other hand, he started with his wholesale price for blank mortgages (2d each), then added five shillings for the binding, he would have charged £2/13 for the register.[67]

---

[66] Cf. Douglas C. McMurtrie, *The Price of Printing in Philadelphia, 1754* (Chicago: Privately Printed, 1928). The document printed by McMurtrie is reprinted in Lawrence C. Wroth, *The Colonial Printer* (New York: The Grolier Club, 1931), pp. 152-153.

[67] Having thought that the Snider volume binding might have cost 6 or 7 shillings, I revised this estimate after consulting with Mr. Willman Spawn. I thank him for this assistance.

On the lower of these estimated retail prices, Franklin and Meredith would have grossed 6½d per perfected sheet; on the higher, 8d per sheet. In order to estimate their profit on whichever of these rates most closely approximates their charge for the register, Franklin needed to deduct the cost of the sheet and the labor for three operations: setting into type prose sufficient to cover a portion of one page only, machining both sides of the sheet twice (all four blank bonds on each sheet being printed from the same setting of type), and folding the sheet. (Stitching was covered in the binder's fee.)

The figures for comparison of profitability, then, are 2⅔d per perfected sheet of pamphlet less labor, versus 6½d or more per perfected sheet of mortgage register less a roughly equivalent amount of labor. The substantial difference between the resulting sums was compounded by another fact. The sales rate for the less profitable pamphlet was uncertain, while that of the more profitable sheets of mortgage bonds was certain and instantaneous. By these measures the printing and selling of the 1729 register was thus "a very profitable Jobb."[68]

This brings us to the last question regarding the possibility that the printing of the 1729 register was Franklin's reward for having supported the emission act. Was the commission to print the register "a great Help" to Franklin? In the context of Franklin and Meredith's first two years in business, the figure 6d-8d per perfected sheet might be considered sufficient to characterize the printing of the register as "a great Help" to them—for they were doubtless paid in cash. The commission, however, was a greater help in two ways.

First, the printing of the register entailed the printing of related legal forms, like the bonds with warrants[69] [Miller 10; PHC, PHi, PPAmP] that had to be signed by every Pennsylvanian who mortgaged his or her property under the 1729 emission act.[70] As such, it was an opportunity for Franklin and Meredith to increase their business's revenues immediately through the sale of small, inexpensive items for which there was a known demand. Franklin made the best of this opportunity by turning again to scrivener Joseph Breintnall, the friend whose assistance had secured the partners the best job of their first year in business.

More than forty years later Franklin still remembered that in 1729 Breintnall helped him publish "Blanks of all Sorts the correctest that ever

---

[68] Cf. George Simpson Eddy, *Account Books Kept by Benjamin Franklin: Ledger 1728-1739; Journal 1730-1737* (New York, 1928), pp. 33-35.

[69] Variously called "bonds and judgments" [Miller A49] and "bonds and warrants" [Miller A74].

[70] Pennsylvania, *Statutes at Large*, vol. IV, p. 107.

appear'd among us."[71] Franklin and Meredith advertised these blanks among the principal items available in the stationer's shop they opened during the summer or early fall of 1729:

> Bibles, Testaments, Psalters, Psalm-Books, Accompt-Books, Bills of Lading bound and unbound, Common Blank Bonds for Money, Bonds with Judgment, Counterbonds, Arbitration Bonds, Arbitration Bonds with Umpirage, Bail Bonds, Counterbonds to save Bail harmless, Bills of Sale, Powers of Attorney, Writs, Summons, Apprentices Indentures, Servants Indentures, Penal Bills, Promissory Notes &c., all the Blanks in the most authentick Forms, and correctly printed; may be had at the Publishers of this Paper; who perform all other Sorts of Printing at reasonable Rates.[72]

The correctness of these blanks and Franklin's friendships with the local clerks (like Breintnall)[73] and office-holders (like Nicholas Scull)[74] who used them insured good sales. Furthermore, the General Loan Office's use of some of these forms was an endorsement that Franklin, Meredith, or any competent shop clerk could easily transfer to their other printed blanks.

Second, the register was Franklin's first piece of official printing for any arm of the provincial government. As such, it was the opportunity he had sought formally since February 18, 1729. In seeking this first opportunity he had three goals: to demonstrate his ability to produce fine work for the province on demand; to prove (with something more substantial than a broadside) the superiority of his work to Andrew Bradford's; and thereby to break Bradford's lock on government printing.

Awarded the printing of the register, Franklin used the opportunity to great effect. Within three months of presenting the nearly flawlessly printed register[75] to the Loan Office trustees, Franklin and Meredith

---

[71] Franklin, *Writings*, ed. by Lemay, p. 1368.

[72] Franklin, *Papers*, 1:164-165.

[73] For Breintnall's first recorded purchases of Franklin and Meredith's printed forms see Miller A14 and A15.

[74] Nicholas Scull (1687-1761), another friend of Franklin's was, like Breintnall, a member of the Junto. For his first recorded purchases of Franklin and Meredith's printed forms see Miller A5-A12 (purchases totaling £5/5/0).

[75] The last line of the blank mortgage form on p. 73 was poorly inked, did not print well, and therefore was supplied in manuscript by the scrivener. This line is the only one of the Register's 14,178 lines to exhibit so grave a defect. Even with this flaw, the 1729 Register is a *particularly* fine piece of printing for its place and time.

"obtain'd, thro' [Franklin's] Friend [speaker of the Pennsylvania Assembly Andrew] Hamilton" a weightier and more lucrative job: "the Printing of the NewCastle Paper Money." Shortly thereafter, on January 30, 1730, the Pennsylvania Assembly voted to have Franklin and Meredith—rather than Bradford—print the next installment of the Assembly's session laws. This is generally interpreted as the vote that made Franklin and Meredith the Assembly's official printers.[76] Whether or not this interpretation is entirely correct, Franklin and his printing office held this remunerative position for the next thirty-six years.[77]

The answers to all these questions being affirmative, it would appear that Franklin did indeed replace his actual printing of the register with his fanciful printing of the money while writing up an otherwise relatively accurate version of these events. His friends in the Assembly did reward him for publishing *A Modest Enquiry* by influencing the Loan Office trustees to commission him to print the 1729 register. It is more difficult to assert whether Franklin's memory played him false while he wrote up the story forty-two years later, or whether he deliberately altered the detail we have focused on here. We will return to this question at the end of this section. In the meantime:

Franklin and Meredith printed the General Loan Office register and related forms like Miller 10 during several days between August 13 and September 14, 1729. (For an explanation of this time frame, and a further, more tentative, narrowing of it, see section II below.) The partner's typography, inking, and press work were excellent; and unlike Bradford's 1724 New Jersey registers, Franklin and Meredith's carried blank mortgage forms on both sides of each leaf rather than just one, thus using the paper as efficiently as the Loan Office's wholly manuscript register had. If any of the Loan Office trustees had seen Bradford's register, they would have appreciated the superiority of the work Franklin and Meredith executed in response to their own commission.

On September 25 Franklin and Meredith purchased from Samuel Keimer his newspaper, the *Universal Instructor in all Arts and Sciences:*

---

[76] In fact, the vote awarded the partners the printing of the next laws and greatly increased their chances of being chosen to print subsequent jobs. It did not, however, confer any formal title or warrant; nor did Franklin style himself "Printer to the Province" in any of his extant imprints until he printed Miller 129 soon after September 17, 1736.

[77] J.A. Leo Lemay, *Benjamin Franklin: A Documentary History*, 1730: Jan. 30. C. William Miller has emphasized that Andrew Bradford continued to print occasionally for the province in the years following the January 30, 1730 vote (as did William Bradford, Jr. starting in July, 1742) despite the Assembly's preference for Franklin's printing office. Miller, "Franklin's Type: Its Study Past and Present," *Proceedings of the American Philosophical Society*, 99 (1955): 425.

and Pennsylvania Gazette. (Keimer had already sold his printing office to David Harry and was preparing to leave Philadelphia for good.) Franklin changed the newspaper's plan to something more attractive than Keimer had been capable of executing and shortened its title to *The Pennsylvania Gazette*. The new owners published their first issue (no. XL) on October 2 [Miller 8; NN, PHi, PPL].

In the first issue of the *Gazette* Franklin and Meredith advertised that they had not yet published, but "speedily" would, Junto member Thomas Godfrey's almanac for 1730 [Miller 5; no copy known].[78] Six weeks later they advertised their edition of John Meredith's *Short Discourse, Proving that the Jewish or Seventh-Day Sabbath Is Abrogated and Repealed*, a small quarto of five half-sheets: 4to, A-E^2 [Miller 7; NN]. And on November 27 they advertised the second edition of Charles Woolverton's *The Spirit's Teaching Man's Sure Guide* [Miller 12; no copy known] as just published.

Franklin and Meredith's next-to-last large job of 1729 was the printing of paper money for New-Castle, Kent, and Sussex Counties, Delaware [Miller 3; no copies seen]. Prof. Lemay thinks Franklin and Meredith executed this job early in December.[79] They probably printed their final large job of the year, their edition of royal half-sheet blank mortgage bonds for Delaware's General Loan Offices, soon thereafter [Miller 18; DeHi], perhaps while the money was being signed. Evidence that Franklin composed two distinct issues of this edition (one tailored to the Sussex County General Loan Office, another tailored to the Kent County General Loan Office) survives in the edition's sole extant exemplar (see section III, no. 2, below). This fact suggests that the edition comprised three distinct issues—one for each Delaware county.

In the middle of January, 1730, Franklin and Meredith printed a broadside edition of Governor Gordon's January 13 address to the Pennsylvania Assembly, with the Assembly's reply of January 14, and the governor's undated acknowledgment of the reply [Miller 29; PHi]. At the end of the month the Assembly voted to have the partners print the next installment of the province's session laws.[80] But before Franklin and Meredith completed this job (which they did a few days before April 9, 1730, when they advertised the new laws [Miller 24; CtY, DLC, MH-L, NN, PHi, PPL, PU] as "Just Published"), they executed more work for the Pennsylvania General Loan Office.

The opportunity to print another edition of blank mortgage forms

---

[78] Whitfield J. Bell, Jr., *Patriot-Improvers: Biographical Sketches of Members of the American Philosophical Society*, 3 vols. (Philadelphia: APS, 1997-), vol. 1, pp. 62-67, esp. p. 63.

[79] J.A. Leo Lemay, *Benjamin Franklin: A Documentary History*, 1729: post November.

[80] J.A. Leo Lemay, *Benjamin Franklin: A Documentary History*, 1730: Jan. 30.

The 1729 Register &c. in Context

arose at the beginning of 1730, after the Loan Office had emitted its quota of loans under the 1729 act. Of the £30,000 in indented legal tender printed under the act, the trustees had first set aside £4,000 for government expenditures specified in the act. They then emitted the remaining £26,000 in loans of not less than £12/10s nor more than £300 to any one borrower as required by law. By December 8, 1729, the trustees had loaned out £25,971 (all but £29 of the mandated total).[81] At this point they closed the 1729 register, opening it again only to record repayments. Yet they were not done emitting money.

The 1726 emission act was still in force; and it prohibited the sinking of paper bills taken in repayment of any and all General Loan Office loans between January 17, 1725, and January 16, 1731. It required, rather, that such sums be "re-emitted again on securities as aforesaid [i.e. mortgages], and so from time to time until all principal moneys anyways accruing . . .shall be wholly re-emitted."[82] As soon as borrowers under the 1723 acts made scheduled loan payments by turning in bills newly freed up by the 1729 emission, the Loan Office trustees found that they would have to re-emit more of the earlier money on new mortgages.

Until this point Loan Office scriveners had enrolled all mortgages granted under the 1726 act entirely in manuscript. But now the Office had become used to working efficiently with the printed register that Franklin and Meredith had supplied in September, 1729. Therefore, after returning briefly to the wholly manuscript tradition which the Office clerks had adhered to through August, 1729, the trustees or Charles Brockden requested Franklin and Meredith to print up sheets of blank mortgage forms adapted to the 1726 act. Between February 19, 1730 (the date the last 1726 mortgage was enrolled wholly in manuscript), and February 24, 1730 (the date the first of the new printed blanks was used), or soon thereafter, the partners obliged by supplying 26 sheets of blank mortgage forms to serve as a printed continuation of the 1726 register.[83]

---

[81] Pennsylvania General Loan Office Mortgage Register, 1729, pp. 263-264.

[82] Pennsylvania, *Statutes at Large*, vol. IV, pp. 39-40

[83] Pennsylvania General Loan Office Mortgage Register, 1724-1731, pp. 328-329. Historical Society of Pennsylvania, MS Collection no. 902 (Am|.266|vol. 2). I have detected neither any evidence in this register, nor any contemporary external comment on the register, that suggests that the wholly manuscript mortgages in it were considered more "authentic" than the partially printed mortgages that follow them. (As suggested elsewhere in the present study, however, it is *conceivable* that Philadelphia scriveners may have attempted to delay use of partially printed forms for General Loan Office mortgages and registers by disparaging them on a variety of grounds, but this notion is currently merely one of several unsupported hypotheses.) Cf. Thomas Starr, [Letter to the editor], *New York Times*, July 9, 1997, p. A20, col. 3, where Starr asserts (vis-a-vis engrossed and printed versions of the Declaration of Independence) that "in the 18th century, type still carried

Since twenty-four or twenty-five sheets constituted a standard quire of paper (the 1729 register comprised 72 sheets, or three twenty-four sheet quires), a twenty-six sheet quire was generous; on it were printed 104 blank mortgages.

The type-page from which Franklin and Meredith printed this first printed continuation of the 1726 manuscript mortgage register included a preamble and debt payment schedule adapted to the 1726 emission act, rather than the 1729 act. It also included several textual improvements over the 1729 mortgage blanks unconnected with the differences between the two acts. These improvements are additional evidence of the great care with which Franklin executed his earliest work for the province.

Franklin and Meredith's 1729 mortgage register had proved satisfactory. Its forms were—as Franklin later claimed for all of his early blanks—"the correctest that ever appear'd among us,"[84] but they were not perfect. They were not perfectly suitable, for instance, for use by a married couple that jointly mortgaged their property. A Loan Office scrivener discovered this when he enrolled the £176 mortgage of Nathaniel and Ann Poole of Philadelphia on page 48 of the 1729 register. When writing on this page the scrivener had to ink out the final two printed letters in "doth", "*HATH*", and "*DOTH*" in lines 8-9 in order to adapt those wholly printed words for man and wife (for whom "do" and "*HAVE*" were customary). Then he had to squeeze in a manuscript "y" in line 49 to finish converting "_he" to "they", because Franklin had not added sufficient blank space after "_he" in this line. (He knew enough to add an extra space *before* it, but whether for the "s" necessary for independent female property owners, or the initial "t" that would begin the letters' manuscript conversion to "they" is not evident.[85])

Because Franklin corrected these imperfections in the first printed continuation of the 1726 General Loan Office mortgage register, we know that he had learned of them somehow. Either he had walked over to the Loan Office himself to see how the 1729 register was serving his patrons—and there saw that his typesetting had necessitated a few manuscript blots. Or someone from the Loan Office (or a friendly inter-

---

a stigma of inauthenticity because of its indeterminate origin, while handwriting bore a direct trace of the author." Scrutiny of the 1726 Loan Office Register, and other wholly manuscript and partially printed legal documents, and early American attitudes toward them, may shed additional light on Mr. Starr's thesis.

[84] Franklin, *Writings*, ed. by Lemay, p. 1368.

[85] Independent widows took out four of the 264 loans (1.51%) granted under the 1729 emission act: Mary Stevens of Birmingham, Chester County (£35); Sarah Read of Philadelphia—Franklin's mother-in-law (£140); Ann Roberts of Nantwell, Chester County (£300); and Mary Appleton of Philadelphia (£112). Pennsylvania General Loan Office Register, 1729 (Collection Jay Snider), pp. 215, 225, 238, and 249.

mediary like Breintnall) had walked over to "The New Printing Office, near the Market" and told Franklin that his forms could be improved a bit more before he set the next edition in type. In either case, Franklin improved his text in these small ways just before executing his next work for the Pennsylvania General Loan Office.[86] Thus the only textual infelicities noted in the 1729 register stand corrected in Franklin and Meredith's blanks for the 1726 mortgage register: "doth", "*HATH*". and "*DOTH*" reappear as "do__", "*HA__*", and "*DO__*". And "_he" reappears as a long blank without any letters at all, so that scriveners might write in either "he", "she", or "they" with equal convenience. Clearly, just as Franklin considered government business well worth securing, he considered it well worth doing very well.[87]

The Loan Office scrivener filled out the last of the 104 blank mortgage forms in the first printed continuation of the 1726 register on or soon after June 10, 1730.[88] A few days later (on or soon after July 3, 1730) the scrivener began to record additional 1726 re-emission mortgages on a new batch of approximately 30 sheets of blank mortgages that Franklin had recently printed from a new type-setting.[89] Of this edition of 120 blank forms (the second printed continuation of the 1726 register), the Loan Office scrivener completed 41 in manuscript before January 6, 1730/1.[90] He never needed to use the remaining 79 mortgage forms (which are consequently still blank today). Ten days later, on January 16, 1731, the re-emission of bills under the 1726 act ceased according to direction of the act.

During the first six months of 1730 Franklin and Meredith continued to print together. On July 14, 1730, however, they dissolved their partnership: Franklin bought Meredith out (with money he borrowed from William Coleman and Robert Grace), and Meredith went

---

[86] Franklin either had not learned of the need for these particular improvements when he and Meredith printed their blank mortgage bonds for the Delaware emission of paper money [Miller 18] or did not bother to improve his text for that edition. The latter possibility is unlikely. Therefore I posit that he learned of these infelicities after he had printed Miller 18.

[87] Care in even so small a matter as this brings Whitfield J. Bell, Jr.'s epithet for Franklin and his like-minded friends to mind: 'patriot-improvers.' See the preface to Dr. Bell's *Patriot-Improvers: Biographical Sketches of Members of the American Philosophical Society*, op. cit.

[88] Pennsylvania General Loan Office Mortgage Register, 1724-1731, p. 432. Historical Society of Pennsylvania, MS Collection no. 902 (Am|.266|vol. 2).

[89] Pennsylvania General Loan Office Mortgage Register, 1724-1731, p. 433. Historical Society of Pennsylvania, MS Collection no. 902 (Am|.266|vol. 2).

[90] Pennsylvania General Loan Office Mortgage Register, 1724-1731, p. 473. Historical Society of Pennsylvania, MS Collection no. 902 (Am|.266|vol. 2).

on his way.[91] With government printing orders sewn up for the foreseeable future, Franklin prospered apace.

Forty-two years after he first printed for the province of Pennsylvania, Benjamin Franklin began to write his memoirs. Did his memory fail him when he wrote that in 1729 his friends in the Assembly rewarded him with the printing of the money for writing *A Modest Enquiry into the Nature and Necessity of a Paper-Currency*? In retelling stories of their lives all autobiographers constantly elide details both essential and inessential to what they might recognize (if shown documentary evidence) as an historical truth. Part of this process of selection is essential to what we generally consider non-fiction storytelling; part is essential, for many people, to the maintenance of public and even private images of themselves. With reference to stories of their own lives, all people are conscious of some parts of the process, unconscious of others. Franklin was no exception.

Occasionally Franklin's omission or alteration of details helped him craft a story more to his advantage than would a more perfect adherence to a documentary record. In his memoirs, for instance, Franklin told of the end to his partnership with Hugh Meredith before he told of his publication of *A Modest Enquiry*, his consequent reward, and all the other work he accomplished in 1729.[92] In fact, Hugh Meredith worked alongside Franklin all through 1729 and well into 1730. Franklin's signal successes in 1729 were therefore not his alone: he could not have set all the type *and* worked every pull of the press. Meredith may have stumbled, but he also worked. Nothing in the historical record, however, has yet been reasonably adduced to demonstrate whether Franklin consciously distorted such elements of his stories—or whether when he wrote of these events as an old man he accurately related them as they played somewhat inaccurately through his brain.

If Franklin retold this particular story faithfully in 1771 his memory had altered the chronology slightly and changed the identity of the work with which his friends in the Assembly rewarded him. The money and the register were two of many printing jobs executed in Philadelphia near the beginning of Franklin's long career. As a young man in 1729 he had very much wanted to print the money. By the time he was an old man, he may have falsely imagined he had. Such alterations appear to be a common part of our life cycles—more common in some kinds of people than others, but common nonetheless. They will become more useful to biographers after we have studied them systematically.

---

[91] Franklin, *Writings*, ed. by Lemay, p. 1366. Meredith survived two or more decades, but left no trace in the historical record after 1749. We do not know when he died, or where.

[92] Franklin, *Writings*, ed. by Lemay, pp. 1366-1370.

On the other hand, Franklin was perfectly healthy in 1771. Much more than a decade would pass before he began to fail noticeably. His memory may not have played him false at all. He may have considered it simpler—or better story-telling—to tell his readers that he was *asked to print the money* than to write that *he was selected to print a lot of blank forms (all of which together constituted a decent commission) connected with the issuance of mortgages that secured the loan of the money that he had helped bring into circulation.* We may never know which of these scenarios—unintentional or intentional alteration of details—is closer to what actually occurred; but one thing is certain: without deviating much from the documentary record, the story Franklin wrote points an important moral more memorably than many another version might.

To the documentary record of Franklin's career, the discovery of Franklin and Meredith's 1729 General Loan Office Mortgage Register has added a previously unimagined artifact that was an important part of his attempt to become printer to the Assembly. Becoming the Assembly's printer, however, was not Franklin's ultimate goal. Rather, for Franklin, securing provincial printing contracts was but one step toward succeeding in his trade so that he might leave it. For however fine a craftsman Franklin was, however dedicated to his trade, and however industrious he was within it, he did not work solely for the joys of printing. (He was not so foolish, however, as either to disdain or fail to cultivate those joys assiduously.)

From the time he and Meredith established their own printing office, Franklin worked hard in order to acquire as quickly as possible a dependable income from investments on which he could retire as early as possible. His goals were to acquire complete freedom from manual labor, to use as much of his hard-earned leisure as possible to *think* about intriguing and useful topics, and to better himself and the communities in which he lived by implementing the results of his studies, observations, and experiments. The 1729 register and its production epitomize several important aspects of Franklin's regular methods of working to achieve these ends.

To Franklin's way of thinking, individual members of society could not *first* help themselves, *then* help others because, as Esmond Wright has noted, for Franklin "individual action could never occur in isolation."[93] One had to help oneself while helping others. As Franklin wrote in 1748: "When you are good to others, you are best to yourself."[94]

A practical example: within this framework, Franklin's vocation was, for part of his life, printing. So like Shakespeare's cobbler, who

---

[93] Wright, *Franklin of Philadelphia*, 81.

[94] Barbour, *Concordance*, 85.

made his fellow men happy by leading them in celebration through the streets of Rome wearing out their shoes, Franklin helped himself by helping others do good in ways that incidentally increased public recourse to his press and the purchase and use of his printed wares. The benefits accrued incrementally along an ascending double-helix to society and to Franklin, to Franklin and society. And though Franklin's own welfare was of vital importance to himself, he well knew that society was infinitely larger than any individual, and that it was the individual who rose with society's helix, rather than vice-versa.

Having worked hard since childhood to develop a correct, persuasive, and accessible prose style, Franklin was ready to assist in the effort to pass a new paper money act in 1729. He wrote and published *A Modest Enquiry* and was rewarded with some government work. "This was," he later wrote, "another Advantage gain'd by my being able to write."[95] It was, however, a greater advantage to the province at large and its other residents, whose common welfare was buoyed by the new emission. Andrew Bradford promptly earned £80 for printing the money—and yet that too was minor compared to the whole province's gain. (On the other hand, Bradford's printing of the money was, of course, his last governmental hurrah. "When you are good to others, you are best to yourself.")

Franklin's experience within this double helix, and his appreciation of its greatest potential, was one of the reasons why he was ever an advocate of cheerful tax-paying, the duty of a true patriot. Franklin never objected to paying his taxes as he prospered during the sixty years after he secured his first government printing job. He never complained about taxes and never worked to decrease them until the ferocity of colonial American opposition to the stamp tax caught him off guard in 1765. After the Revolution, one of his most widely reprinted shorter works, *Father Abraham's Speech* (alias *The Way to Wealth*), continued to testify to his disdain for destructively thoughtless groaning against taxation.

The idea that virtuous citizens could find a reason to dislike contributing to the maintenance of the common wealth and the government that fostered it shocked him. Taxation that fostered Pennsylvania's growth had paid Franklin for many a printing job. As a virtuous citizen, he endeavored to pay the commonwealth back by executing superior printing for it, by promoting educational and medical institutions, by declining to patent any of his life-improving and life-saving inventions, by serving in elective and appointed office—and not least by trying to establish and promote a model for similar behavior.

There was nothing particularly original about the individual

---

[95] Franklin, *Writings*, ed. by Lemay, p. 1368.

elements of Franklin's involvement with the 1729 emission. Philadelphian Francis Rawle (1660-1727) had written and published a pro-money pamphlet in 1721, the year after the South Sea bubble burst.[96] Rawle intended thereby to bring about the paper money act that was eventually passed in 1723. Franklin's pro-money pamphlet is the more cogent of the two, better written, more accessible, and (judging from the results) more timely. But it was not original in conception or composition. Andrew Bradford had printed loan office registers before Franklin did, but not for Pennsylvania's General Loan Office trustees, who continued to purchase mortgage registers of wholly blank pages after they knew partially printed registers to be an option. Franklin, on the other hand, printed a better mortgage register than Bradford had; and worked with at least one scrivener to insure that it would prove an acceptable instrument for breaking the Loan Office clerks' manuscript tradition.

Franklin's involvement in the 1729 emission was original in that he, a young tradesman, here brought together so many disparate elements of participation in civic life, and infused each with such thoughtful care. Whether composing an accessible political tract that turned on complicated economic concepts, setting an essay into type as a "mere mechanic," conversing persuasively with his patron Andrew Hamilton or his fellow tradesman Joseph Breintnall, or composing, inking, and proofing a mundane printed blank, Franklin recognized the value and the rewards of careful planning and superior work. The 1729 mortgage register epitomizes the care Franklin expended on the genesis and execution of his early government commissions. On one level, he was only trying to stay in business—a result devoutly wished for, but by no means assured.[97] Yet on another level, he was orchestrating the first deal of a business relationship that he hoped would enable him to retire some day, and in retirement to contribute something to the world's store of practical philosophy.

---

[96] Francis Rawle, *Some Remedies Proposed, for the Restoring the Sunk Credit of the Province of Pennsylvania* ([Philadelphia:] Printed [by Andrew Bradford] in the year, 1721) [Evans 2287; PPL, RPJCB].

[97] Franklin's attempt to co-opt the serious competition he feared he faced in David Harry (Samuel Keimer's successor) by asking Harry to join him in partnership indicates how concerned Franklin was in 1729 that competition might soon destroy his business.

II
Evidence for the Precise Dating of the 1729 Register and the First & Second Printed Continuations of the 1726 Register

The evidence supporting ranges of dates within which we can be reasonably certain Franklin and Meredith printed, first, the 1729 General Loan Office Register and, subsequently, the two distinct continuations of the 1726 Register requires a detailed explanation. This is particularly so because at first glance it would appear reasonable to posit that blank mortgage bonds with texts adapted to the 1726 emission act were printed before those with texts adapted to the 1729 act.

Two characteristics of the printed continuations of the 1726 Register, however, prove that they were not printed in 1726, nor indeed before August 1729. First, they were printed with Franklin and Meredith's type, which did not reach Philadelphia until 1728. Second, the printed texts of both editions of the 1726 mortgage blanks specify "*Samuel Carpenter, Jeremiah Langhorne, William Fishbourn* and *Philip Taylor*" as the trustees of the General Loan Office. These trustees did not serve together until sometime in August, 1729, when Philip Taylor replaced deceased trustee Nathaniel Newlin (who had served as a trustee with the other three since 1723).[98]

But because the 1729 mortgages, as well as both editions of the 1726 blanks, name Carpenter, Langhorne, Fishbourn, and Taylor as Loan Office trustees, the presence of Taylor's printed name on the forms only proves that none of these editions was printed before August, 1729. It does not help establish the order in which the three editions were composed and printed off. Nor do the manuscript dates that Loan Office scriveners inscribed on any of these forms have evidentiary value regarding the order in which the editions were printed.[99] The mortgages could have been *used* in an order different from that in which they were printed.

The following paragraphs examine the evidence that establishes the

---

[98] Pennsylvania, *Statutes at Large*, vol. 3, p. 325; vol. 4, p. 101.

[99] In fact, most of the manuscript dates in the registers do not even prove an absolute *terminus ad quem* for the printing of the several editions. The dates on the enrolled mortgages are scriveners' copies of the dates written on the engrossed mortgages; and the scriveners may have copied them a few days later.

Evidence for Dating

order in which these editions were printed and the ranges of dates within which they were produced.

1. Sequence

Two kinds of bibliographical evidence establish the order in which Franklin and Meredith printed these editions: typographical, and textual. The typographic evidence is sufficient to establish conclusively the order in which the three editions were printed. Textual evidence, which is sometimes considered less conclusive than typographic evidence, corroborates the typographic evidence—and vice-versa.[100]

Franklin and Meredith used a single, ornate cast heading of the words "This Indenture" at the top of all three of these mortgage forms. This heading (called here cast heading A) was made of cast type metal (an alloy of lead, antimony, tin, and a small percentage of copper). Letters and ornaments made of type metal maintain their shape under the padded, even pressure of regular fingering and press work. They sustain nicks and bends, however, when pressed against harder objects like grit (which sometimes blows into ink) or clumsily stuck with a printer's bodkin during routine work. If damaged on its face (the surface that was inked to leave its impression on paper), a piece of type, ornament, or cast heading leaves different impressions before and after the damage occurred.

Cast heading A left slightly different impressions in the mortgages under consideration here. In all of the 1729 mortgage forms, the topmost flourish over the right side of the letter "T" in "This" is unbroken, while the flourish over the letter "h" in the same word exhibits one hairline break at about 3 o'clock. In all of the blank mortgage forms constituting the first printed continuation of the 1726 register the topmost flourish over the right side of the letter "T" in "This" is broken at 12 o'clock and the flourish over the letter "h" is broken by two thin lines around 3 o'clock. This is evidence that cast heading A was not damaged at all above the "T" until after Franklin and Meredith had finished printing the 1729 register; and that it had already been damaged there, and that the damage to the flourish around the "h" had been doubled before they began to print the first edition of mortgages adapted to the 1726 emission

---

[100] That the textual evidence corroborates the typographic evidence—and vice-versa—is useful to know because of the number of bibliographic problems in which textual evidence is plainer than typographic evidence, or in which typographic evidence alone is inconclusive.

act. In other words, this variant establishes beyond question that Franklin and Meredith printed the 1729 register before they printed the first continuation of the 1726 mortgage register. The textual improvements over the 1729 mortgage blanks present in the first edition of forms adapted to the 1726 emission act corroborate this typographic evidence (see section I above).

In all of the mortgage forms constituting the second printed continuation of the 1726 register the topmost flourish over the right side of the letter "T" in "This" is broken at 12 o'clock just as it is in the forms of the first continuation mortgages. But in the second continuation, damage to the flourish over the letter "h" at 3 o'clock differs from the damage evinced in the first continuation. Where the flourish over the "h" is damaged in the first continuation by two thin breaks, it is broken in all of the second continuation forms *by a 2 mm. gap*. In other words, after the printing of the first continuation and before the printing of the second continuation the small piece of type metal between the two thin breaks in the flourish over the letter "h" broke off, leaving a 2 mm. gap in the flourish at 3 o'clock. This variant establishes beyond question that Franklin and Meredith printed the second continuation after they printed the first.

A pair of textual variants in the second continuation of the 1726 similarly establishes that its blank mortgage form was set into type and run through the press after those in the first continuation. While setting type for the first continuation, Franklin set the year in which he thought the mortgages would be engrossed and enrolled as "One Thousand Seven Hundred and [blank]" (line 2) and "*Anno Domini* 17 [blank]" (line 42). He set the years this way because when he and Meredith printed off this edition of forms neither they nor anyone in the Loan Office knew when the Loan Office scriveners would finish using them. That is, Breintnall, Franklin, and the Loan Office staff knew enough to suspect that if Franklin typeset the year as "One Thousand Seven Hundred and Twenty-Nine" and "*Anno Domini* 1729", some months later Loan Office scriveners might have to blot out "Twenty-Nine" and "29" and squeeze their manuscript versions of "Thirty" and "30" in between neatly printed lines of otherwise correct words. This suggests that Franklin thought he set these types to produce mortgage blanks that would be used in both 1729 (or 1729/30, i.e. the first three months of what we now call 1730) *and* 1730 (April-December of what they called, and we still call simply

1730).¹⁰¹

The type-page used to print the *second* continuation of the 1726 register, on the other hand, included the dates "One Thousand Seven Hundred and Thirty [blank]" (line 2) and "*Anno Domini* 173[blank]" (line 42). This indicates that Franklin knew that none of the mortgages in this edition would be used in 1729 or 1729/30. He anticipated rather that all the blank mortgage forms in this edition would be used in the 1730s (though not in just *one* year in the 1730s). Because we are not free to speculate that the *first* continuation of the 1726 register may have been printed in, say, 1739/40, this also demonstrates that the second continuation of the 1726 register was printed after the first. That is, the typographical and textual evidence concur that the two continuations of the register were printed in the order in which they were used.

2. Ranges of dates

The date on which Philip Taylor officially replaced the deceased Nathaniel Newlin as a trustee of the General Loan Office is the *terminus a quo* for the printing of the 1729 mortgage register. The sources, however, have not yet yielded up that date, but only a date before which Taylor could not have replaced Newlin. And yet that date is not the day Newlin died.

According to a 1730 Pennsylvania law that includes a terse historical summary of the first Loan Office trustees' tenure, Philip Taylor "was nominated a trustee in [Nathaniel Newlin's] stead" when Newlin died sometime in May, 1729 (the very month during which Newlin was reappointed trustee by the 1729 emission act).¹⁰² But Taylor's succession to Newlin's Loan Office position did not occur this promptly. The *Votes and Proceedings of the House of Representatives of the Province of Pennsylvania* record the following facts:

After the governor signed the 1729 emission act on May 10, the House adjourned until August 11. During its morning session on August 12, the House officially learned that one of the Loan Office trustees [i.e.

---

¹⁰¹ Franklin had also thought this when he set the 1729 mortgage form into type. At that time, apparently neither he nor Loan Office officials were certain the entire 1729 emission would be loaned out before January 1729/30.

¹⁰² Pennsylvania, *Statutes at Large*, vol. 4, p. 190 ("An Act to Remove the Trustees of the General Loan Office of Pennsylvania and Appointing Others to Execute the Said Trust"); Horle, and others, *Lawmaking & Legislators in Pennsylvania*, vol. 1, p. 564 (approximate date of Newlin's death).

Newlin] had died. On the afternoon of the twelfth, Loan Office trustee William Fishbourn waited on the House and informed it "that the [Loan Office] Trustees had chosen *Richard Hayes* a Trustee, in the Room of *Nathaniel Newlin*, deceased; and pray'd Leave of the House till Tomorrow to produce the Credentials of his [i.e. Hayes's] Qualifications." The House debated Fishbourn's request before granting it. Fishbourn, however, soon to be disgraced for embezzling Loan Office funds (and staging a burglary to attempt to cover up his crime), did not return to the House the following day, nor do the *Votes and Proceedings* record any further discussion on the Loan Office trustees' choice of Hayes or of the Assembly's subsequent decision to pass over Hayes in favor of Taylor.[103]

It therefore appears that even if Hayes served (at most) as trustee *de facto* from Newlin's death until sometime after Fishbourn notified the House of the fact, the House never recognized Hayes as a trustee. Rather, the House appointed Philip Taylor sometime after Fishbourn told them that "the Trustees had chosen *Richard Hayes* a Trustee" to replace Newlin. Then in 1730 the House summarized the *de jure* succession to Newlin thus: "in the year one thousand seven hundred and twenty-nine, Nathaniel Newlin, one of the said trustees, died, and one Philip Taylor, of Chester County, was nominated a trustee in his stead."[104] Since Hayes's name does not appear printed on any of the mortgages, the mortgages could not have been printed until after his brief *de facto* tenure as trustee had ended (if it had ever really begun). Nor could the mortgages have been printed before August 12, 1729, when the House discovered that Fishbourn et al "had chosen *Richard Hayes*".

The 1729 emission act called for £30,000 in indented legal tender Loan Office Bills to be issued September 15, 1729. The earliest mortgage enrolled in the 1729 Register (p. 8) was executed and witnessed September 23, 1729. Therefore Franklin and Meredith probably printed these bonds between the beginning of Philip Taylor's trusteeship (sometime after August 12, 1729) and the date of the first mortgages—probably before the date set by law for the emission of the bills of credit.

Two additional considerations may justify a further narrowing of this window. First, Franklin is unlikely to have executed such an important job at the last minute. The register itself confirms this in the present instance: it does not bear any stigmata of hasty work. Second, the House is unlikely to have resolved the question of Newlin's succession

---

[103] *Votes*, p. 1964-1965.

[104] Pennsylvania, *Statutes at Large*, vol. 4, p. 190.

Evidence for Dating

immediately after Fishbourn told them the trustees had chosen Hayes. It is therefore likely that Franklin and Meredith printed the 1729 mortgage forms within the period August 20-September 6. This hypothesis allows the week of September 8-13 for the Philadelphia bookbinder William Davies to bind the 72 sheets of mortgage forms sturdily within the leather-covered paste-boards that still protect the register's sheets today.

As to the two printed continuations of the 1726 mortgage register: the preponderance of circumstantial evidence suggests that the mortgage forms constituting each of the continuations were printed shortly before the first one of each edition was used.[105]

As noted above in section I, Loan Office scriveners last enrolled a mortgage granted under the 1726 act wholly in manuscript on (or soon after) February 19, 1730. On (or soon after) February 24, 1730, a scrivener first used Franklin and Meredith's first printed continuation of the 1726 register to enroll the next recorded 1726 mortgage. Therefore the partners probably set this first continuation in type from a marked copy of their 1729 mortgage form and printed its 26 sheets during that three-working-day interval (February 20, 21, 23; February 22 was a Sunday), or during four work days beginning February 19 or soon thereafter. The work is unlikely to have consumed more than a small portion of each work day; but the machining of each sheet four times, with time for drying after each, may have been spread out over that many days.

The last mortgage enrolled in the first printed continuation is dated June 10, 1730. The first enrolled in the second continuation is dated July 3, 1730. For reasons discussed earlier in this section, we know that Franklin set the blank mortgage form used to print the second continuation knowing that it would not be used before April, 1730. The partners, then, probably printed these bonds between March and July, 1730. It is possible that they did not print them until May or June, when the Loan Office trustees are likely to have become aware that they would soon need additional mortgage forms adapted to the 1726 Act.

---

[105] No edition of blank mortgage bonds that was printed long before one of its exemplars was first used has been discovered. See a related minor emendation to Prof. Miller's note on Miller 139 under number 8 in section III below.

III
Franklin & Meredith's (1728-1730), Franklin's (1730-1748), and Franklin & Hall's (1748-1766) Mortgage Bond Printing: Additions to Miller

The three editions of blank mortgage forms printed by Franklin and Meredith for the Pennsylvania General Loan Office in 1729 and 1730 and examined in the previous sections of this article are the only forms of this sort yet located that C. William Miller did not discover or learn of during his work on *Benjamin Franklin's Philadelphia Printing*. During the decades Prof. Miller devoted to Franklin's bibliography, the 1729 Register was held somewhere in private hands—most likely all unawares; and both editions of mortgage blanks adapted to the 1726 emission act were hidden at the back of a manuscript volume at the Historical Society of Pennsylvania.[106]

Prof. Miller was the first historian of an American printing office to conduct a systematic survey of ephemeral productions of his subject's press. He did not, however, include in his bibliography full entries for every one of the distinct printed blanks he attributed to Franklin and Meredith's, Franklin's own, and then Franklin and Hall's press. Rather he published complete descriptions of representative blanks, with full attention to paper and type (as in Miller entries 10, 18, and 30 under date 1729 and 1730), and included in the annexed notes the locations of some similar blanks.[107] Thus, in his entries for the blank mortgage forms Franklin and Meredith printed for Delaware's Kent County General Loan Office [Miller 18] and the blank New Jersey mortgage bonds they

---

[106] The Historical Society of Pennsylvania's General Loan Office Register of Indentures (1724-1730) is not catalogued as a partially-printed document in the most recent finding aid, which post-dates publication of *Benjamin Franklin's Philadelphia Printing* by seventeen years. *Guide to the Manuscript Collections of the Historical Society of Pennsylvania* (Phila.: HSP, 1991), collection # 902.

[107] Prof. Miller's report *sub* Miller 18 of General Loan Office mortgage bonds printed by Franklin or Franklin and Hall extant in "the Real Estate Office, Dept. of Internal Affairs, Harrisburg, Pa." may have originated in an overly optimistic report from the Pennsylvania State Archives. According to the *Pennsylvania Manual*, the Department of Internal Affairs (which was abolished in 1968) never oversaw an agency called "the Real Estate Office." Nor have I found in State Archives Record Group 14 (Dept. of Internal Affairs) any papers labeled "Real Estate Office." State Archives Record Group 8 (General Loan Office) does not include any records generated before 1773. However, RG 8 does include four partially printed folio mortgage registers dating 1774-1788 that might easily have been mistaken for Franklin bonds.

printed later in the 1730s [Miller 135], Prof. Miller recorded where his readers would find similar, later mortgage forms.

Except for its first, third, and fourth items, then, the following list merely follows Prof. Miller's suggestions for further research. The format of each entry here follows Prof. Miller's format as well, so that his readers may travel easily between the 856 main entries in part one of *Benjamin Franklin's Philadelphia Printing* and the sixteen items described below.

A note on measurements: Tradition suggests that sheet dimensions be given in inches and tenths of inches and I have followed Prof. Miller in applying these units to leaf size as well. Allan Stevenson's system for measuring watermarks in millimeters has had few followers. I have attempted to be one of them, partly so that I might have the pleasure of recommending his articles as among the most delightful in bibliographical literature.

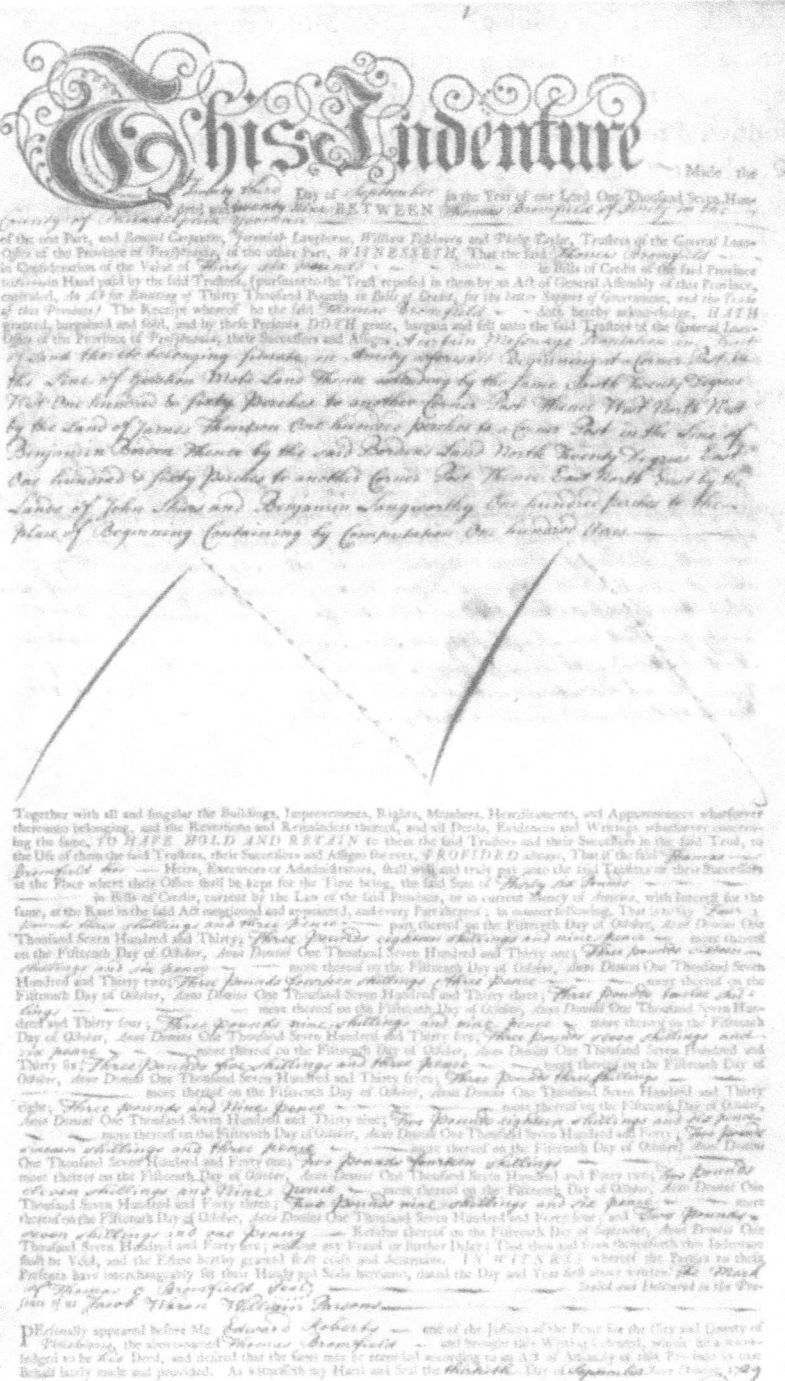

No. 1. Courtesy Jay Snider.

Additions to Miller

1. PENNSYLVANIA GENERAL LOAN OFFICE MORTGAGE REGISTER FOR THE 1729 EMISSION.

PENNSYLVANIA. General Loan Office. This Indenture. Mortgage Bond printed for loans given "pursuant to the Trust reposed in them [i.e. the Loan Office trustees, "*Samuel Carpenter, Jeremiah Langhorne, William Fishbourn* and *Philip Taylor*"] by an Act of General Assembly of the Province of Pennsylvania, entituled, *An Act for Emitting of* Thirty Thousand Pounds *in Bills of Credit, for the better Support of Government, and the Trade of this Province*".

[No imprint] [1729: ~August/September]

COLLATION: Royal 2° A^4(-$A4$) B-I^4(-$I1$) K-$2E^4$($2E2+\chi 1[=2M3]$) $2F$-$2G^4$(-$2G1,2$) $2H^4$(-$2H1$) $2I$-$2M^4$(-$2M3$). 139 leaves, paged in contemporary manuscript through $2K4^v$, 1-264; final seven leaves unpaged.

TEXT: 51 lines. 401 x 216 mm.

TYPE: BF pica no. 1.

PAPER: Imported sheets, at least 23 x 18.18 in., marked Strasbourg bend (119 x 16[10|27|10]16 mm.) | IV. The paper in this volume is homogeneous and was manufactured with a pair of molds most easily differentiated by the positions of their countermarks: in one mold the V was pushed into the nearest chainline, largely merging its right arm with the chain; in the other, the V is well-formed—only the serif atop its right arm touches the nearest chain.

LEAF: 18.18 x 11.5 in. (462 x 292 mm.)

REFERENCES: None located.

NOTES: Attributed to BF's press on the type evidence. Franklin cast heading A (solid letters; state 1: topmost flourish over the right side of the letter T in "This" unbroken; flourish over the letter h in "This" scarcely broken by one hairline break just below 3 o'clock). Whether this cast heading was Franklin's first, or one of two distinct cast headings he had in his office in September 1729 may someday be answered. At this writing it is only possible to state that Franklin's use of this cast heading predates by five or six months his use of the cast heading that appears in Miller 18.

When this register was first bound it comprised 72 sheets of royal paper, or 144 folio leaves with 288 blank mortgage forms. Regarding the first five canceled leaves noted in the collation statement, we can safely posit either (1) that imperfections in one of the two mortgage blanks on leaves *A*4, *I*4, 2*G*1,2, and 2*H*1 necessitated their removal before the register was delivered to the Loan Office, or (2) that Loan Office scriveners made serious errors in enrolling mortgages on those leaves and therefore excised them before beginning afresh on the next leaves. The former possibility is less likely than the latter for several reasons, not least of which is that Franklin would have caught and removed sheets with serious imperfections before he delivered them to the binder. Therefore it seems more likely that the Loan Office scrivener canceled them while he was working in the register. (Because the pages of enrolled mortgages were numbered sequentially soon after they were completed, we know that none of these leaves was canceled at a later date.)

The Loan Office scrivener excised the sixth and final cancel (leaf 3*M*3) sometime after he realized that he had neglected to enroll a pair of mortgages in their proper order (approximately by date) in signature 2*E*. He rectified the error by excising 3*M*3 from the back of the register and tipping it into the middle of signature 2*E*. The identity of the leaf added to signature 2*E* as the leaf excised from signature 3*M* is established by the watermark evidence and the measurement of prick marks present in signature 3*M* and the single in question.

Three small dots of red sealing wax survive on the stub from which leaf *I*1 was cut. This suggests that the scrivener may have tried earlier to move another leaf (perhaps 2*G*1, 2*G*2, or 2*H*1) to replace that excised leaf, but that its failure to adhere necessitated its destruction.

COPY: Jay Snider.

2. MORTGAGE BONDS FOR THE 1729/30 DELAWARE EMISSION.
DELAWARE. Kent County. General Loan Office. This Indenture. Mortgage Bond printed for loans given "pursuant to the Trust reposed in them [i.e. *"Mark Manlove* and *Richard Richardson . . Trustees* of the *General Loan-Office* of the said County of *Kent"*] by an Act of General Assembly of the said Government, entituled, *An Act for the Emitting and making Current, the Sum of Twelve Thousand Pounds in Bills of Credit"*.
[No imprint]   [1729: ~December]

COLLATION: Royal half-sheet.
TEXT: 51 lines. 383 x 220 mm.
TYPE: BF pica no. 1.
PAPER: Imported, marked Strasbourg bend. This is the same stock Franklin used to print the 1729 register and the first and second continuations of the 1726 register. See paper note under no. 1 above.
LEAF: 18.4 x 11.9 in.
REFERENCES: Miller 18.
NOTES: Attributed to BF's press on the evidence of the type and cast heading. Franklin cast heading B (formerly identified as Franklin's first cast heading). Although the Delaware Historical Society's copy is the only exemplar of any issue of this edition of mortgage bonds located to date, it is probably one of three distinct issues. The erroneous printing of *"Sussex"* at the end of line 48 of the present issue, in which the printed text is otherwise correctly adapted to the Kent County General Loan Office (lines 4 and 5), appears to have been overlooked by the compositor when he revised, for the present issue, the type-page set for the preceding issue. Whether the supposititious issue for New-Castle County preceded or followed those for Sussex and Kent may be determined if additional exemplars of the edition are ever discovered. Exemplars of the New-Castle County and Sussex County issues have not yet been located.

Because the law to which these bonds are adapted was passed at the end of October, 1729 (J.A. Leo Lemay, *Benjamin Franklin: A Documentary History*, © 1997 [www.english.udel.edu/lemay/franklin/], 1729: 30 October), these bonds could not have been printed before the beginning of November, 1729. On the other

No. 2. Courtesy Historical Society of Delaware.

hand, the imperfect readings "doth", "*HATH*", and "*DOTH*" in line 10 (see section I above) strongly suggest that this edition was printed before Franklin learned of the minor difficulties these readings had occasioned during use of the 1729 Pennsylvania mortgage register. Since Franklin corrected these reading in his first continuation of the 1726 Pennsylvania register (no. 3 below), he and Meredith probably printed the present bonds in December, 1729, or January 1729/30.

COPIES: DeHi.

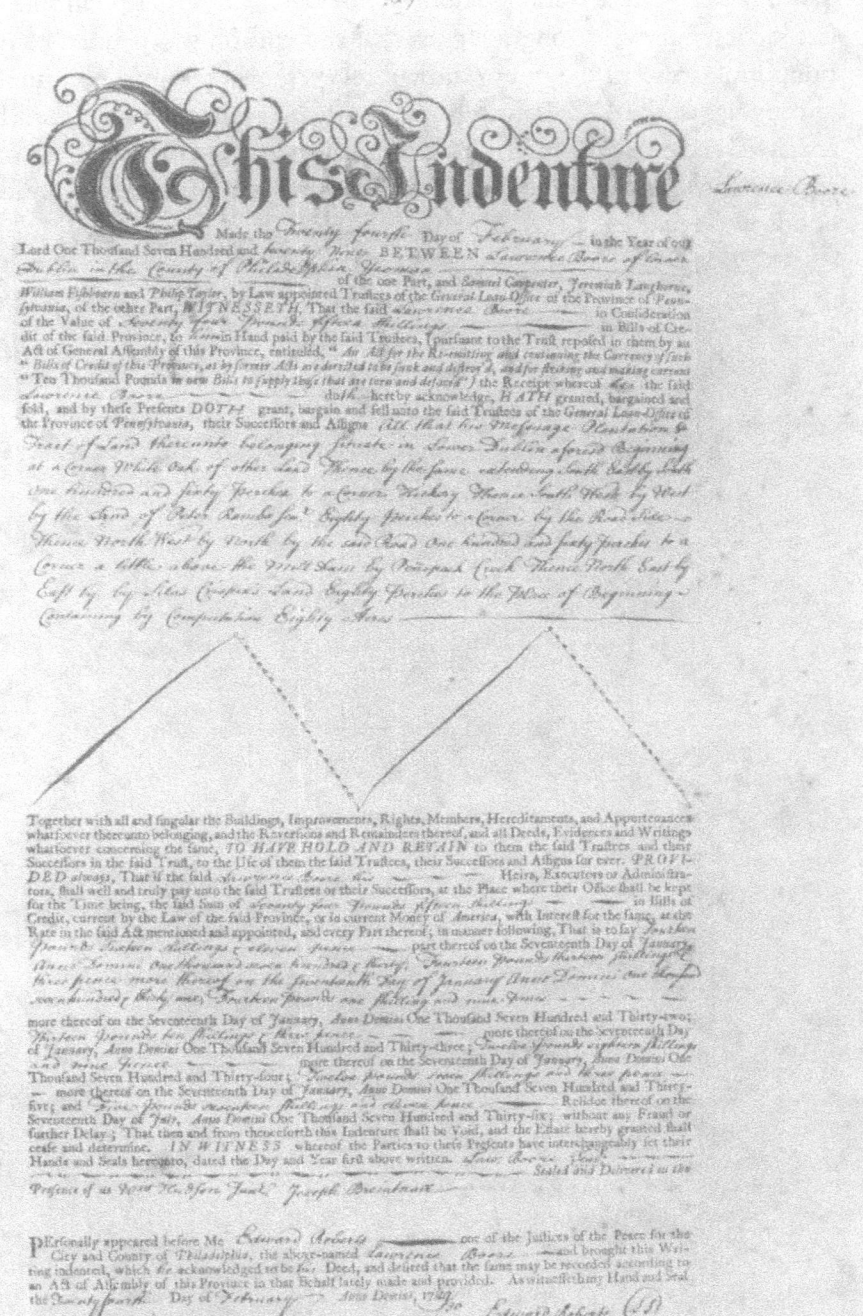

No. 3. Courtesy the Historical Society of Pennsylvania.

3. First Printed Continuation of the Pennsylvania General Loan Office Mortgage Register for the 1726 Re-emission.

PENNSYLVANIA. General Loan Office. This Indenture. Mortgage Bond printed for loans given "pursuant to the Trust reposed in them [i.e. the Loan Office trustees, "*Samuel Carpenter, Jeremiah Langhorne, William Fishbourn* and *Philip Taylor*"] by an Act of General Assembly of this Province, entituled, "*An Act for the Re-emitting and continuing the Currency of such* | *"Bills of Credit of this Province, as by former Acts are directed to be sunk and destroy'd, and for striking and making current* | *"Ten Thousand Pounds in new Bills to supply those that are torn and defaced"*.

[No imprint]   [1730: ~February]

COLLATION: Royal 2° in fours. 52 leaves paged in contemporary manuscript 329-432, rebound in a General Loan Office register for 1724-1731. Signatures and number of cancels undetermined.

TEXT: 42 lines. 371 x 196 mm.

TYPE: BF pica no. 1.

PAPER: Imported sheets, at least 23 x 18.17 in., marked Strasbourg bend (119 x 16[10|27|10]16 mm.) | IV. This is the same stock Franklin used to print the 1729 register. See paper note under no. 1 above.

LEAF: 18.17 x 11.5 in.

REFERENCES: None located.

NOTES: Attributed to BF's press on the evidence of the type and cast heading. Franklin cast heading A (solid letters; state 2: topmost flourish over the right side of the letter T in "This" broken at 12 o'clock; flourish over the letter h in "This" broken *by two thin lines* at 3 o'clock). The trustees whose names are printed in this and the second version of the 1726 bond did not serve together until after Philip Taylor's appointment as trustee sometime after August 12, 1729. Although adapted to the 1726 Act, these bonds were therefore printed after Newlin's death. The damaged loop over the h in the cast heading indicates further that these bonds were printed after the 1729 bonds, which Franklin printed with the same cast heading before it had been damaged in that spot. Neither line 2 nor line 42 includes the decade in their printing of the year ("One Thousand Seven Hundred and [blank]" in the former, "*Anno Domini* 17 [blank]" in the latter). For a discussion of the dating and textual superiority of these blank mortgage forms to those constituting the 1729 Register, see sections I and II above.

COPY: PHi.

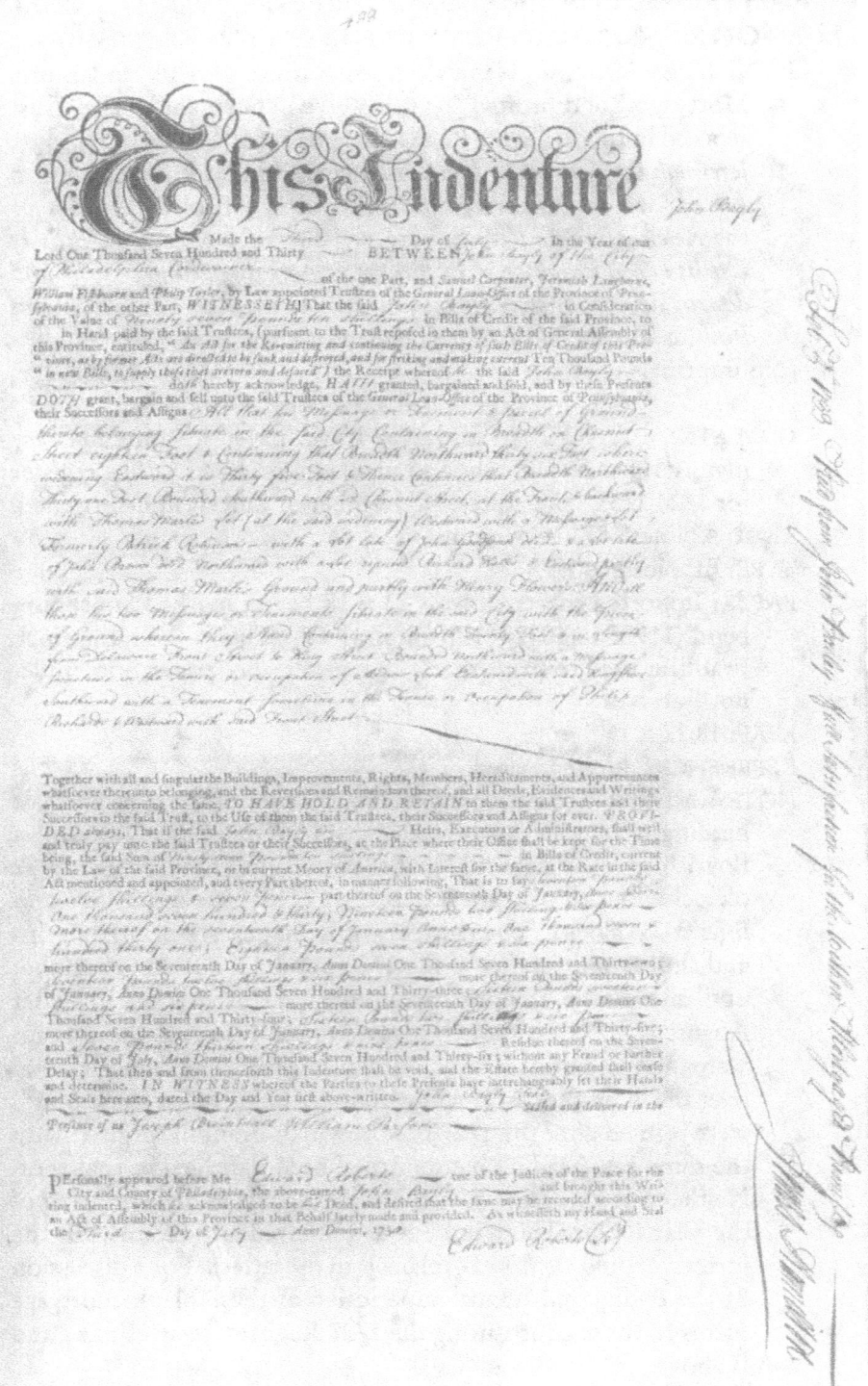

No. 4. Courtesy the Historical Society of Pennsylvania.

Additions to Miller

4. SECOND PRINTED CONTINUATION OF THE PENNSYLVANIA GENERAL LOAN OFFICE MORTGAGE REGISTER FOR THE 1726 RE-EMISSION.

PENNSYLVANIA. General Loan Office. This Indenture. Mortgage Bond printed for loans given "pursuant to the Trust reposed in them [i.e. the Loan Office trustees, "*Samuel Carpenter, Jeremiah Langhorne, William Fishbourn* and *Philip Taylor*"] by an Act of General Assembly of this Province, entituled, "*An Act for the Re-emitting and continuing the Currency of such Bills of Credit of this Pro-*| "*vince, as by former Acts are directed to be sunk and destroyed, and for striking and making current* Ten Thousand Pounds| "*in new Bills, to supply those that are torn and defaced*".

[No imprint]　　　　　　　　　　　　　　[1730: ~May-June]

COLLATION: Royal 2° in fours. 60 leaves, of which the first 21 are paged in contemporary manuscript 433-474, while the next 39 are unpaged leaves of blank forms; rebound in a General Loan Office register for 1724-1731. Signatures and number of cancels undetermined.

TEXT: 42 lines. 371 x 195 mm.

TYPE: BF pica no. 1.

PAPER: Imported sheets, at least 23 x 18.17 in., marked Strasbourg bend (119 x 16[10|27|10]16 mm.)| IV. This is the same stock Franklin used to print the 1729 register and the first continuation of the 1726 register. See paper note under no. 1 above.

LEAF: 18.17 x 11.5 in.

REFERENCES: None located.

NOTES: Attributed to BF's press on the evidence of the type and cast heading. Franklin cast heading A (solid letters; state 3: topmost flourish over the right side of the letter T in "This" broken at 12 o'clock; flourish over the letter h in "This" broken *by a 2 mm. gap* at 3 o'clock). Second setting of the text composed for mortgages drawn up in conformity with the 1726 Act. As in the first setting, the trustees named are those who did not serve together until after Philip Taylor's appointment as trustee sometime after August 12, 1729. In this setting, however, lines 2 and 42 include the decade in their printing of the year, thus: "One Thousand Seven Hundred and Thirty [blank]" in the former, "*Anno Domini* 173 [blank]" in the latter. For a discussion of the dating and textual superiority of these blank mortgage forms to those constituting the 1729 Register, see sections I and II above.

COPY: PHi.

No. 5. Courtesy the Bucks County Historical Society.

Additions to Miller

5. 1733 MORTGAGE BONDS FOR THE 1731 RE-EMISSION. SEPARATE SETTING.

PENNSYLVANIA. General Loan Office. This Indenture. Mortgage Bond printed for loans given "pursuant to the Direction of an Act of General Assembly of this Province, made in the Fourth Year of the Reign of His Majesty King *GEORGE the Second*, over *Great-Britain*, &c. entituled, *An Act for Re-emitting and Continuing the Currency of such Bills of Credit of this Province as by former Acts are directed to be sunk and destroyed*".

[No imprint]   [1733]

COLLATION: Folio broadsheet, verso blank.
TEXT: 51 lines. 395 x 237 mm.
TYPE: BF pica no. 1.
PAPER: Imported sheet, at least 16.25 x 12.8 in., marked Arms of Amsterdam (113 x 13[12|25|24.5|25.5|14]11 mm.)| IML. Cf. the paper used in Miller 63: *Articles of Agreement* (1733).
LEAF: 16.25 x 12.8 in.
REFERENCES: See notes *sub* Miller 18.
NOTES: Attributed to BF's press on the evidence of the type and cast heading. Franklin cast heading A (solid letters; state 3: topmost flourish over the right side of the letter T in "This" *probably* broken at 12 o'clock [entire defect not visible in the only located exemplar]; flourish over the letter h in "This" broken by a 2 mm. gap at 3 o'clock). Trustees named in print: "*Andrew Hamilton, Charles Read, Jeremiah Langhorne, Richard Hayes*, and *John Wright*."

The exemplar at the Bucks County Historical Society (Blackfan-Dawson Collection | MSC 9, Fol. 4) is completed in manuscript for John Dawson of Solebury, dated February 7, 1733/4, and docketed on the verso "Copy of | John Dawson's | Mortgage | pr new Reemitt.^{g} act".

COPY: PDoHi.

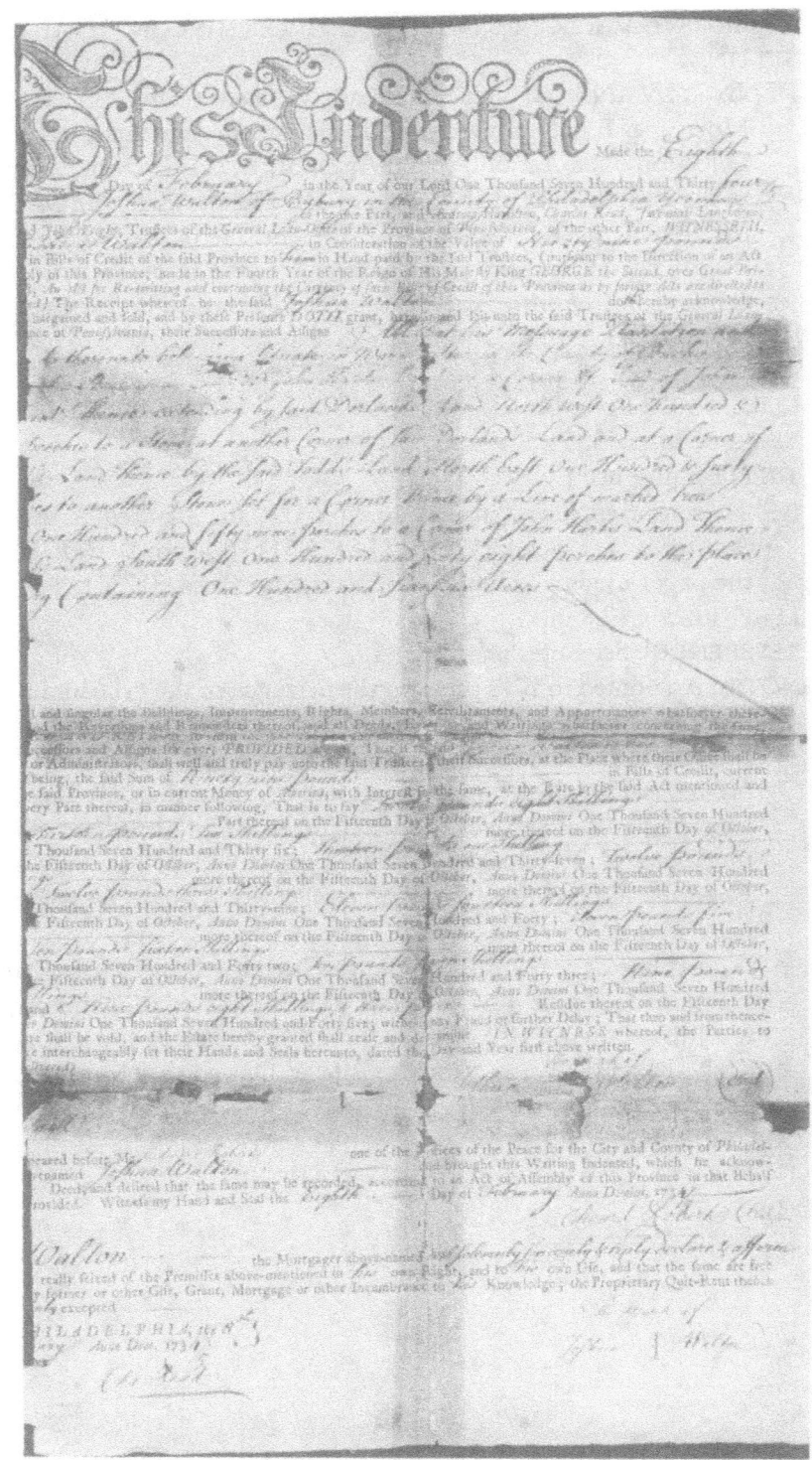

No. 6. Courtesy the Bucks County Historical Society.

Additions to Miller

6. 1734 MORTGAGE BONDS FOR THE 1731 RE-EMISSION. SEPARATE SETTING.

> PENNSYLVANIA. General Loan Office. This Indenture. Mortgage Bond printed for loans given "pursuant to the Direction of an Act [of General Assem]bly of this Province, made in the Fourth Year of the Reign of His Majesty King *GEORGE the Second*, over *Great-Bri*[*tain*, &c. entitule]d, *An Act for Re-emitting and continuing the Currency of such Bills of Credit of this Province as by former Acts are directed to* [*be sunk and destroy*]*ed"*.
> [No imprint] [1734]

COLLATION: Folio broadsheet, verso blank.
TEXT: 49 lines. 389 x ___ mm. *Lacks left-hand portion.*
TYPE: BF pica no. 1.
PAPER: Imported sheet, at least 16.25 x ___ in., marked Arms of Amsterdam (113 ? x 10[14|25.5|24|24|13.5]10.5 mm.) | IML. Cf. the paper used in Miller 63: *Articles of Agreement* (1733).
LEAF: 16.25 x ___ in.
REFERENCES: See notes *sub* Miller 18.
NOTES: Attributed to BF's press on the evidence of the type and cast heading. Franklin cast heading C (letters horizontally hatched; state 1: topmost flourish over the right side of the letter T in "This" undamaged and smoothly rounded; flourish over the letter h in "This" broken at 3 o'clock). Trustees named in print: "*Andrew Hamilton, Charles Read, Jeremiah Langhorne,* [*Richard Hayes*?], *and John Wright."*

This bond is the earliest printed with Franklin's cast heading C yet located. The forms of its letters and the shape and details of its flourishes are nearly identical to cast heading A. The letters in cast heading C, however, are horizontally hatched and the second downstroke in the letter h in "This" curves beneath and to the left of the nadir of the first downstroke. (By 1733, the second downstroke in the letter h in "This" in cast heading A stops short of the nadir of the first downstroke). Although cast heading C nearly duplicates cast heading A in general appearance, it consumed less ink per impression because of the hatching of its letters.

The exemplar at the Bucks County Historical Society (Hattie Ann Walton Family Papers, folder 1: Deeds & Mortgages) is completed in manuscript for Joshua Walton of Bybury, mortgagor, dated February 8, 1734, and docketed in manuscript on the verso "Joshua Walton's | Mortgage | pr New Reemittg Act".
COPY: PDoHi.

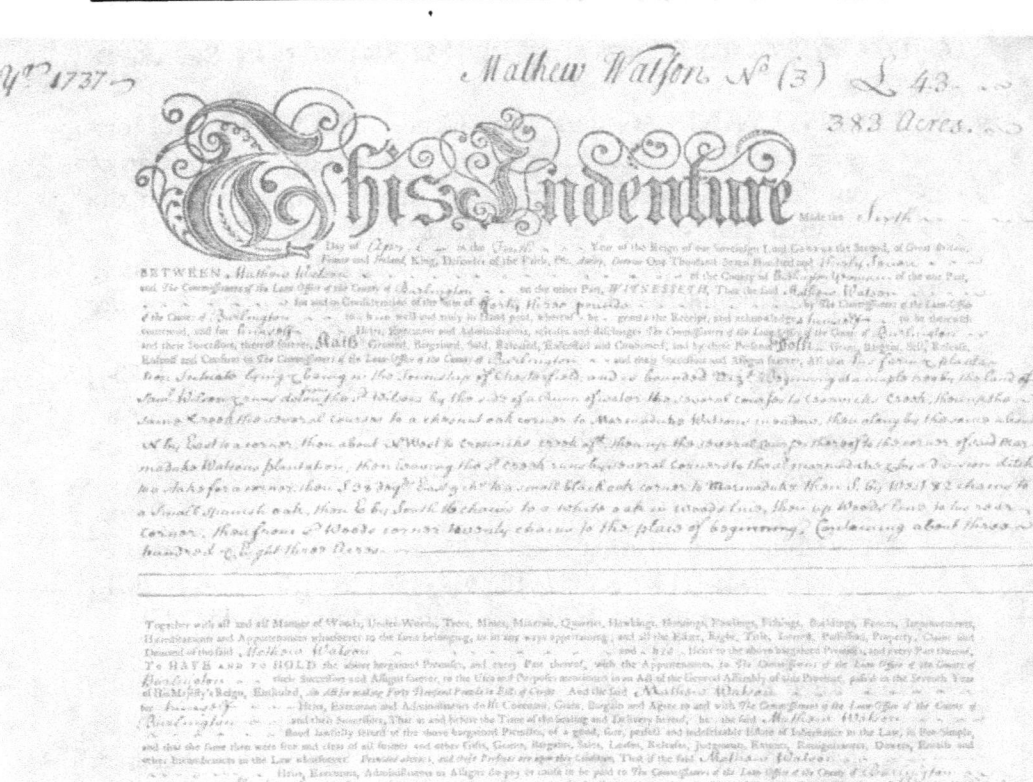

No. 7. Courtesy New Jersey State Archives.

Additions to Miller

7. 1737 NEW JERSEY COUNTY LOAN OFFICE MORTGAGE REGISTERS.
NEW JERSEY. Loan Office of the County of [blank]. This Indenture. Mortgage Bond printed by direction of "an Act of the General Assembly of this Province, pass'd in the Seventh Year of His Majesty's [i.e. George the Second] Reign, Entituled, *An Act for Making Forty Thousand Pounds in Bills of Credit*".
[No imprint]   [1737]

COLLATION: Foolscap folio broadsheets, 289 in the Burlington County register, 203 in the Hunterdon County register. Number of cancels undetermined.
TEXT: 53 lines. 333 x 241 mm.
TYPE: BF long primer no. 1.
PAPER: Imported sheets, at least 15.9 x 12.4 in., marked Arms of Amsterdam | H.
LEAF: 15.9 x 12.4 in.
REFERENCES: Miller 135.
NOTES: Ascribed by Miller to BF's press on the evidence of the cast heading and type. Franklin cast heading C (letters horizontally hatched; state 1: topmost flourish over the right side of the letter T in "This" undamaged and smoothly rounded; flourish over the letter h in "This" broken at 3 o'clock).

    The loan act to which these forms were tailored was passed on August 16, 1733. The sixteen-year loans, however, were not given until March 25, 1737, sometime after the King had approved the Act, which specified that the Loan Officers of ten New Jersey counties "shall be provided with Books of Blank Mortgages, printed and bound up" (Bush, comp., *Laws of the Royal Colony of New Jersey, 1703-1745*, pp. 474-487; quotation, p. 486). The books for Burlington (289 broadsheets) and Hunterdon (203 broadsheets) counties are at the New Jersey State Archives, Trenton (County Records, Burlington, Loan Office, Mortgage vol. 3 [1737-1750]; and County Records, Hunterdon, Loan Office, Mortgage vol. C [1737-1748]). Bound at the front of each book are six narrow folio leaves designed to be used for an index of mortgagors' names; at the outer margin of the index rectos, the alphabet is printed vertically with BF's French canon no. 1 titling types (cap. 11.5cm.), the letters inked alternately in black and red.
COPIES: Nj.

No. 8. Courtesy the American Philosophical Society.

8. 1737 MORTGAGE BONDS FOR THE 1731 RE-EMISSION. SEPARATE SETTING.

PENNSYLVANIA. General Loan Office. This Indenture. Mortgage Bond printed for loans given "pursuant to the Direction of an Act of General Assembly of this Province, made in the Fourth Year of the Reign of His Majesty King *GEORGE the Second*, over *Great-Britain*, &c. entituled, *An Act for Re-emitting and Continuing the Currency of such Bills of Credit of this Province as by former Acts are directed to be sunk and destroyed*".

[No imprint] [1737]

COLLATION: Folio broadsheet, verso blank.
TEXT: 47 lines. 378 x 240 mm.
TYPE: BF pica no. 1.
PAPER: Imported sheet, at least 16.5 x 13.1 inches, marked Pro Patria (95 x 0[24.5|24.5|24.5|24.5]0 mm)| crown GR.
LEAF: 16.5 x 13.1 in.
REFERENCES: Miller 139.
NOTES: Ascribed by Miller to BF's press on the evidence of the cast heading and type. Franklin cast heading C (letters horizontally hatched; state 2: topmost flourish over the right side of the letter T in "This" nicked at 12 o'clock and slightly flattened; flourish over the letter h in "This" broken at 3 o'clock). The use in this edition of cast heading C in state 2 disproves Miller's supposition that these bonds "could have been printed at any point in the earlier 1730's." They could not have been printed until after Franklin had printed the extant 1737 New Jersey mortgage registers (no. 7, above).

The PPAmP exemplar (MSS: B/F86L/oversize) is completed for Robert and Mary Jordan, mortgagors, dated November 16, 1737, and docketed in manuscript on verso, "Copy| Rob^n Jordan & Ux. [. . .]| Mort^{ge}| p Reemit^s Act of 1731". (This mortgage is recorded on p. 210 of the General Loan Office register for 1736-38 [Philadelphia City Archives, spine no. 1402].)
COPY: PPAmP.

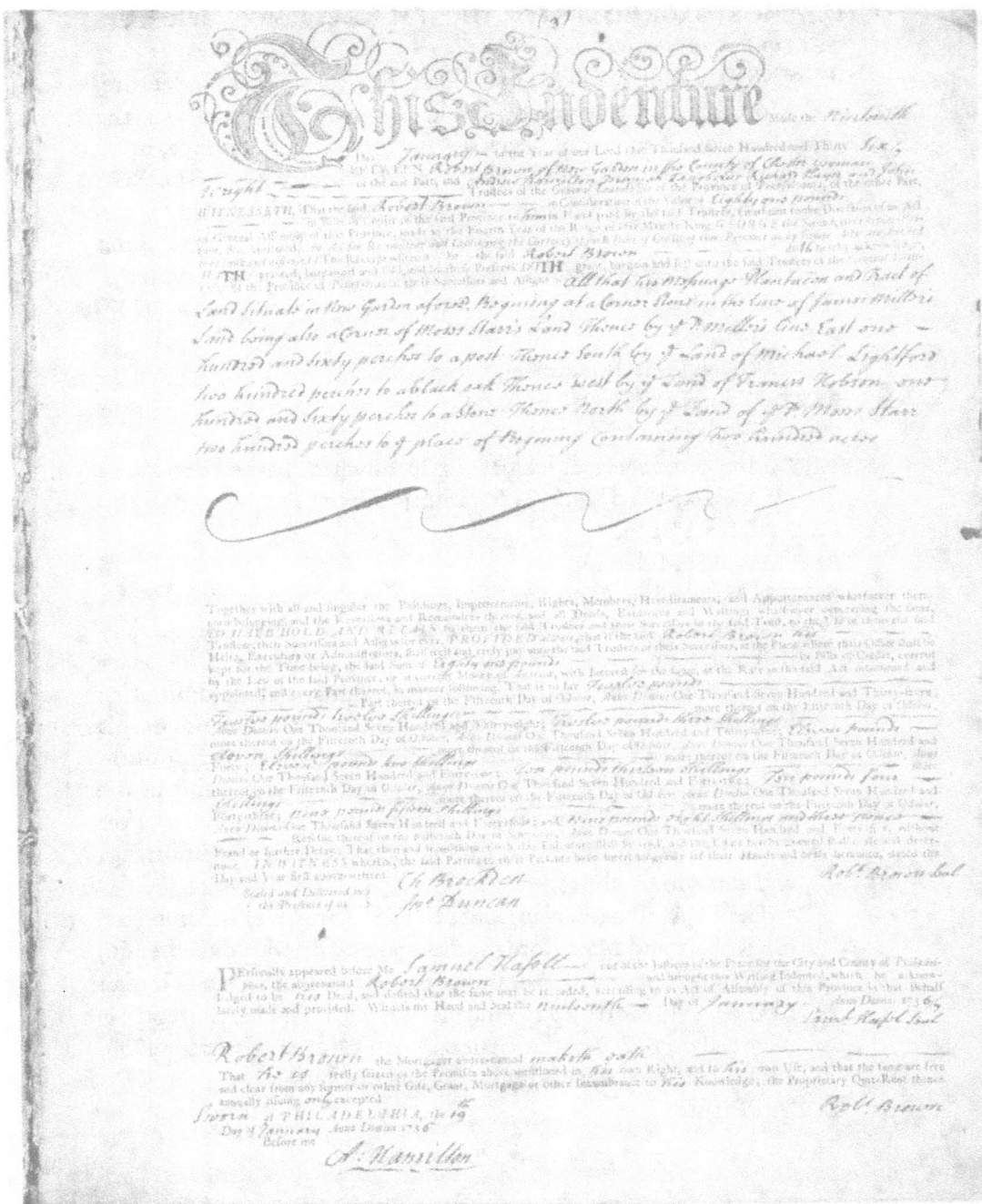

No. 9. Courtesy the City of Philadelphia, Dept. of Records, City Archives.

9. 1737 PENNSYLVANIA GENERAL LOAN OFFICE MORTGAGE REGISTER FOR THE 1731 RE-EMISSION.
PENNSYLVANIA. General Loan Office. This Indenture. Mortgage Bond printed for loans given "pursuant to the Direction of an Act of General Assembly of this Province, made in the Fourth Year of the Reign of His Majesty King *GEORGE the Second*, over *Great-Britain*, &c. entituled, *An Act for Re-emitting and Continuing the Currency of such Bills of Credit of this Province as by former Acts are directed to be sunk and destroyed*".
[No imprint] [1737]

COLLATION: Folio broadsheets, versos blank. At least 217 copies bound up into a mortgage register; number of cancels undetermined.

TEXT: 48 lines. 375 x 240 mm.

TYPE: BF pica no. 1.

PAPER: Imported sheets, at least 15.9 x 12.5 in., marked Arms of Amsterdam (89 x 15[10|25|24|25|11]14 mm.)| crown GAS; with three random sheets (leaves 63, 77, and 78) indistinctly marked Arms of Amsterdam (100 x ? mm.)| ——DEL (*perhaps* I IANDEL ?; cf. paper used in Miller 199: New Jersey, *Votes and Proceedings*, 1740).

LEAF: 15.9 x 12.5 in.

REFERENCES: Cf. Miller 139.

NOTES: Attributed to BF's press on the evidence of the type and cast heading. Franklin cast heading C (letters horizontally hatched; state 2: topmost flourish over the right side of the letter T in "This" nicked at 12 o'clock and slightly flattened; flourish over the letter h in "This" broken at 3 o'clock). Lines 2 and 47 include the decade in their printing of the year, thus: "One Thousand Seven Hundred and Thirty [blank]" in the former, "*Anno Domini* 173[blank]" in the latter. One of 197 duplicate forms of at least 217 (lacking nos. 1, 2, 4, 6, 7, 10, 12, 14, 17, 18, 20, 22, 24, 26, 28, 30, 35, 37, 60, and 124; no. 118 is loose but present) once bound in the General Loan Office register for 1736-1738 (Philadelphia City Archives spine number 1402). The mortgage recorded on the first extant page (p. 3) is the earliest mortgage in this volume and is dated in manuscript January 19, 1736/7; the mortgage on the final extant page (p. 217) is dated March 15, 1737/8; the latest mortgage, however, is dated May 9, 1738 (p. 201). The mortgages are recorded in approximate chronological order (with several exceptions) through p. 201, after which mortgages running from October 15, 1737 to March 15, 1737/8 appear on pp. 202-217.

Charles Read's name ceases to appear in manuscript on these forms as a trustee on December 8, 1736, suggesting that he was incapacitated by illness from this point until his death, which occurred on January 6, 1737 (Horle and others, 2: 881). *The Pennsylvania Gazette* of January 13, 1737, reported that Read died "On Thursday last . . .after a lingering illness."

COPIES: Philadelphia, Department of Records, City Archives.

10. 1739 MORTGAGE BONDS FOR THE 1739 RE-EMISSION AND FURTHER STRIKING OF £11,110/5S. SEPARATE SETTING (WIDE).
PENNSYLVANIA.   General Loan Office.   This Indenture. Mortgage Bond printed for loans given "pursuant to the direction of of [sic] an Act General Assembly of this Province, made in the *Twelfth* Year of the Reign of his Majesty King *GEORGE the Second*, over *Great Britain, &c.* entitled, *An ACT for Re-printing, Exchanging and Re-emitting all the Bills of Credit of this Province, and for striking the further Sum of* Eleven Thousand One Hundred and Ten Pounds Five Shillings, *to be emitted upon Loan*".
[No imprint] [1739]

COLLATION: Folio broadsheet, verso blank.
TEXT: 40 lines. 399 x 326 mm.
TYPE: BF pica no. 2.
PAPER: Imported sheet, at least 19.8 x 15 in., marked Strasbourg lily LVG (130 x 7[17.5|25|17.5]7 mm.) | IV (cf. Churchill 406).
LEAF: 19.8 x 15 in.
REFERENCES: None located.
NOTES: Attributed to BF's press on the evidence of the type and cast heading. Franklin cast heading C (letters horizontally hatched; state 2: topmost flourish over the right side of the letter T in "This" nicked at 12 o'clock and slightly flattened; flourish over the letter h in "This" broken at 3 o'clock). Neither line 2 nor line 39 includes the decade in its printing of the year, thus: "One Thousand Seven Hundred and [blank]" in the former, "*Anno Domini* 17 [blank]" in the latter.

Textual errors in these bonds are the earliest substantive errors yet discovered in mortgage blanks printed in Franklin's office. Corrupt readings mar three lines of these bonds: "of one part" (for "of the one part") in line 2; "of of an Act General Assembly" in line 5; and "whereof he said" (for "whereof he the said" in line 7. Franklin repeated this last error in no. 11, corrected it in 12, but then repeated it again in nos. 13 and 14 (which we can therefore posit were set from a copy of 10 or 11). This error is also repeated in the unattributed ca. 1741 mortgage bonds for the 1739 re-emission [Loan Office Register for 1745-1747; Philadelphia, Department of Records, City Archives, spine no. 1405] and the unattributed ca. 1746 mortgage bonds for the 1746 re-emission [rebound in General Loan Office register for 1741-1747; Philadelphia, Department of Records, City Archives], though in

No. 10. Courtesy the American Philosophical Society

both of these it appears with a slightly lengthened space after "_he". This error is repeated in a 1749 mortgage register for the 1746 re-emission tentatively attributed to William Bradford, Jr. [rebound in the Loan Office Register for 1747-1742, Philadelphia, Department of Records, City Archives], which suggests that Bradford used a marked Franklin bond for copy when he printed it from badly set types in 1749 (unless Bradford also printed the ca. 1741 mortgage bonds for the 1739 re-emission and the ca. 1746 mortgage bonds for the 1746 re-emission, in which case he used a marked Franklin bond as copy for the ca. 1741 mortgage bonds for the 1739 re-emission, and then reiterated the error on his own in the ca. 1746 mortgage bonds for the 1746 re-emission and the 1749 mortgage register for the 1746 re-emission). And Franklin and Hall modified the error without correcting it in our no. 15, thus: "the Receipt whereof he [blank] said [blank]". Thus, it appears that over the course of a decade, a typographical error in one of Franklin's 1739 mortgage blanks became accepted legal language amongst General Loan Office trustees and clerks.

The PPAmP exemplar (B/F86L/oversize) is the original mortgage, completed in manuscript for Robert and Mary Jordan, mortgagors, on October 15, 1740, and carries the autograph signatures of Richard Armitt and John Bringhurst as witnesses to the mortgage. (This mortgage is recorded on p. 485 of the General Loan Office register for 1739-1741 [Philadelphia City Archives spine no. 1403], where the witnesses' signatures are secretarial copies.)

COPY: PPAmP.

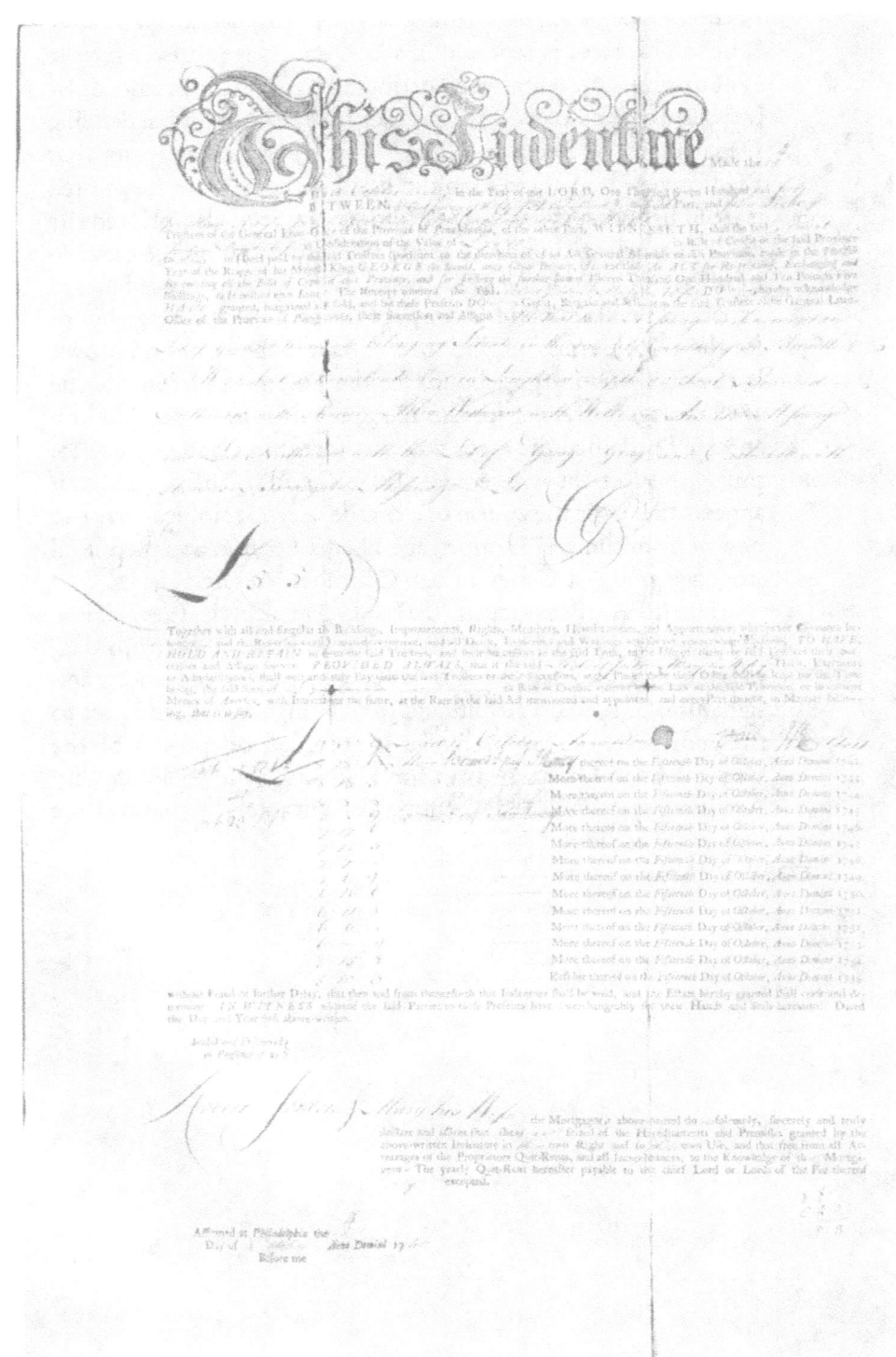

No. 11. Courtesy the American Philosophical Society

Additions to Miller

11. 1739 MORTGAGE BONDS FOR THE 1739 RE-EMISSION AND FURTHER STRIKING OF £11,110/5S. SEPARATE SETTING (NARROW).
PENNSYLVANIA.   General Loan Office.   This Indenture. Mortgage Bond printed for loans given "pursuant to the direction of of [sic] an Act General Assembly of this Province, made in the *Twelfth* Year of the Reign of his Majesty King *GEORGE the Second*, over *Great Britain, &c.* entitled, *An ACT for Re-printing, Exchanging and Re-emitting all the Bills of Credit of this Province, and for striking the further Sum of* Eleven Thousand One Hundred and Ten Pounds Five Shillings, *to be emitted upon Loan*".
[No imprint]   [1739]

COLLATION: Folio halfsheet, verso blank.
TEXT: 47 lines.   415 x 238 mm.
TYPE: BF pica no. 2.
PAPER: (1) PPAmP: Imported sheet, at least 23.8 x 18.25 in., marked IV. (2) PDoHi: fragment marked Strasbourg bend.
LEAF: 18.25 x 11.9 in.
REFERENCES: See notes *sub* Miller 18.
NOTES: Attributed to BF's press on the evidence of the type and cast heading. Franklin cast heading C (letters horizontally hatched; state 2: topmost flourish over the right side of the letter T in "This" nicked at 12 o'clock and slightly flattened; flourish over the letter h in "This" broken at 3 o'clock). Neither line 2 nor line 47 includes the decade in its printing of the year, thus: "One Thousand Seven Hundred and [blank]" in the former, "*Anno Domini* 17[blank]" in the latter.

Corrupt readings mar three lines: (1) "of one part" (for "of the one part") in line 3; (2) "of of an Act General Assembly" in line 6; and (3) "whereof _he_ said" (for "whereof _he_ the said") in line 9. Lines 20-33 are leaded. This form is likely to have been printed in late 1739 (see note under 12, below).

The PDoHi fragmentary exemplar (Armitage Collection, MSC 2, Fol. 5; top half of mortgage bond only) is completed for James Hamilton, dated June 11, 1740, and docketed in manuscript on verso "Copy|James Hamiltons | Mortgage | p £80000 Act of 1739".

The PPAmP exemplar (B/F86L/oversize), completed in manuscript for Robert and Mary Jordan, mortgagors, unwitnessed and dated October 15, 1740, is docketed in manuscript on the verso "Copy| Robert Jordon & Mary his Wife| Mortgage| p £80000 Act".
COPIES: PDoHi, PPAmP.

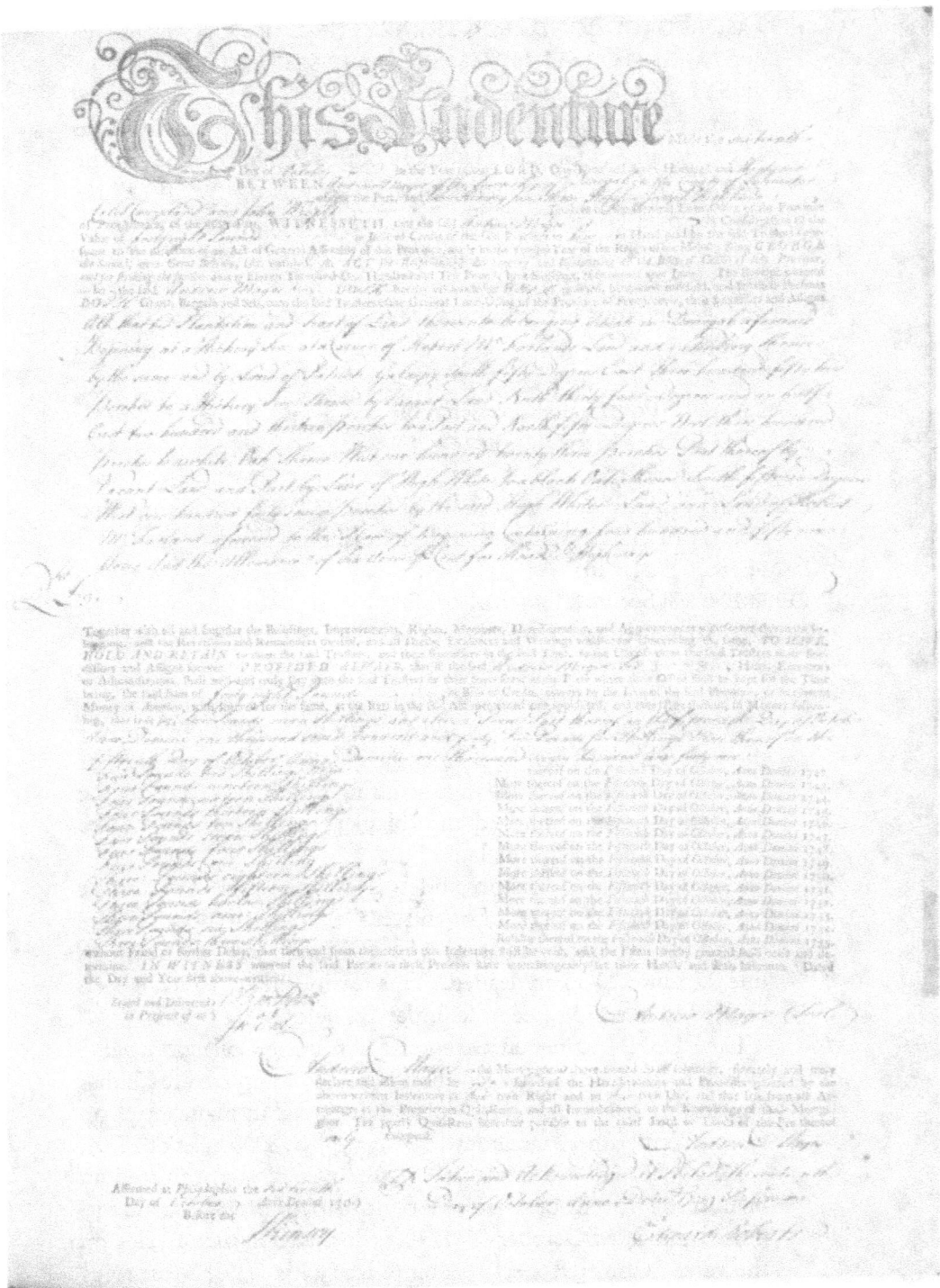

No. 12. Courtesy the City of Philadelphia, Dept. of Records, City Archives.

Additions to Miller

12. 1739 PENNSYLVANIA GENERAL LOAN OFFICE MORTGAGE REGISTER FOR THE 1739 RE-EMISSION AND FURTHER STRIKING OF £11,110/5s.

PENNSYLVANIA. General Loan Office. This Indenture. Mortgage Bond printed for loans given "pursuant to the direction of an Act of General Assembly of this Province, made in the *Twelfth* Year of the Reign of his Majesty King *GEORGE the Second*, over *Great Britain, &c.* entitled, *An ACT for Re-printing, Exchanging and Re-emitting all the Bills of Credit of this Province, and for striking the further Sum of* Eleven Thousand One Hundred and Ten Pounds Five Shillings, *to be emitted upon Loan*".

[No imprint]   [1739]

COLLATION: Folio broadsheet, printed in duplicate on recto and verso. At least 290 copies bound up into a mortgage register; number of cancels undetermined.

TEXT: 48 lines. 388 x 241 mm.

TYPE: BF pica no. 2.

PAPER: Imported sheets, at least 16.2 x 12.25 in., marked Pro Patria (94 x 5[19|25|25|26|19]6 mm.)| IV.

LEAF: 16.2 x 12.25 in.

REFERENCES: See notes *sub* Miller 18.

NOTES: Attributed to BF's press on the evidence of the type and cast heading. Franklin cast heading C (letters horizontally hatched; state 2: topmost flourish over the right side of the letter T in "This" nicked at 12 o'clock and slightly flattened; flourish over the letter h in "This" broken at 3 o'clock). Neither line 2 nor line 47 includes the decade in its printing of the year, thus: "One Thousand Seven Hundred and [blank]" in the former, "*Anno Domini* 17 [blank]" in the latter.

    Three corrupt readings present in no. 11 (above) are emended in the present type-setting as follows: (1) the corrupt reading "of one part" (for "of the one part") in line 3 of no. 11 is miscorrected here in line 4 to "of one the part"; (2) the corrupt reading "of of an Act General Assembly" in line 6 of no. 11 is corrected here in line 8 to "of an Act of General Assembly"; (3) the corrupt reading "whereof _he_ said" in line 9 of no. 11 is corrected here in lines 10-11 to "whereof| _he_ the said".Lines 21-34 are unleaded.

    One of 290 broadsheets, all printed recto and verso, now rebound in the General Loan Office register for 1739-1741 (Philadelphia City Archives spine number 1403). The leaves are paged 1-582 in contemporary manuscript; one leaf, pp. 285-6, has been excised, but reduced copies from microfilm of these two mortgages are loosely inserted in the volume. The earliest mortgage (p. 1) is dated October 2, 1739; the latest (p. 582) is dated June 10, 1741.

COPIES: Philadelphia, Department of Records, City Archives.

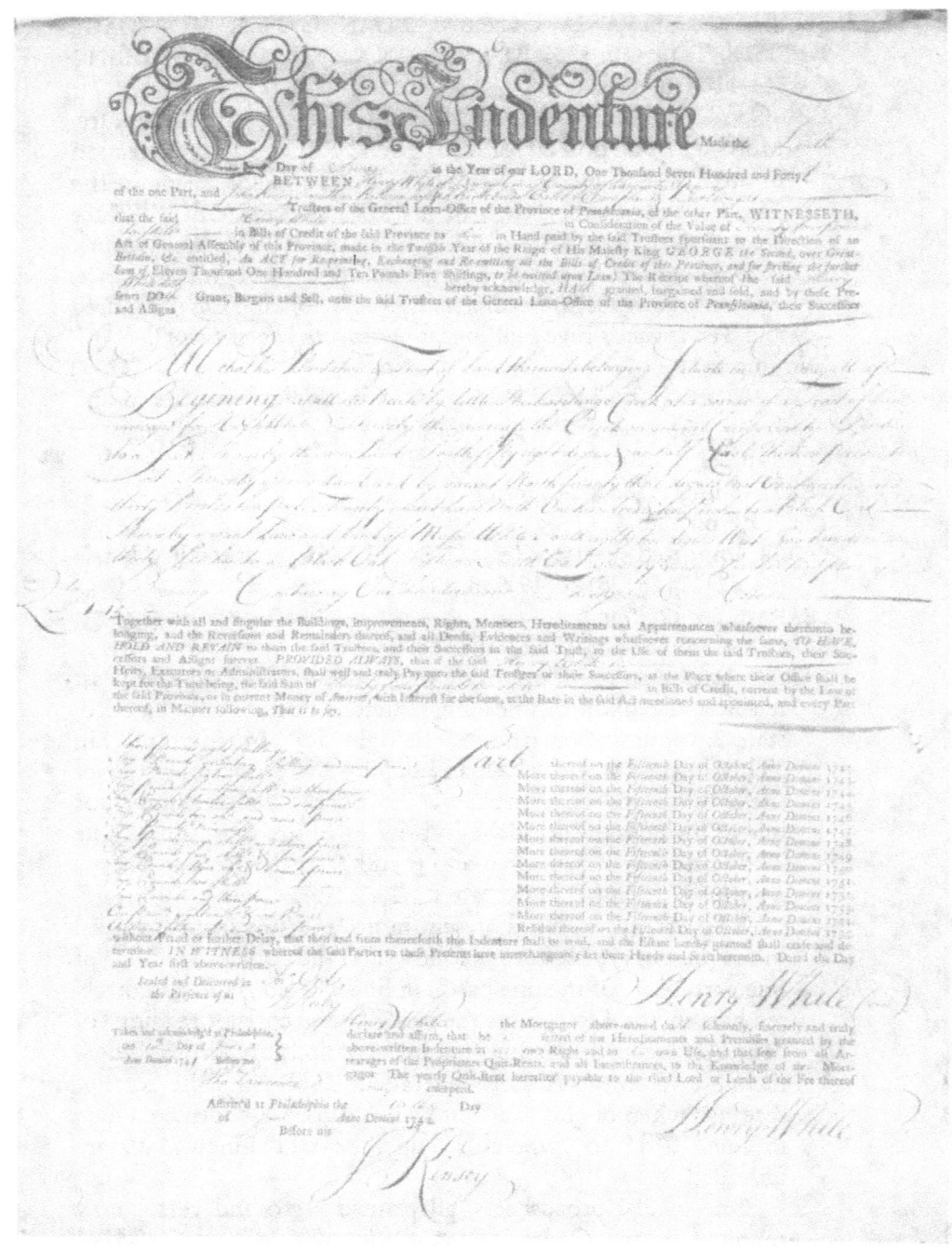

No. 13. Courtesy the City of Philadelphia, Dept. of Records, City Archives.

13. 1740 PENNSYLVANIA GENERAL LOAN OFFICE MORTGAGE REGISTER FOR THE 1739 RE-EMISSION AND FURTHER STRIKING OF £11,110/5s.
PENNSYLVANIA. General Loan Office. This Indenture. Mortgage Bond printed for loans given "pursuant to the Direction of an Act of General Assembly of this Province, made in the *Twelfth* Year of the Reign of His Majesty King *GEORGE the Second*, over *Great-Britain, &c.* entitled, *An ACT for Re-printing, Exchanging and Re-emitting all the Bills of Credit of this Province, and for striking the further Sum of* Eleven Thousand One Hundred and Ten Pounds Five Shillings, *to be emitted upon Loan*".
[No imprint]   [1740]

COLLATION: Folio broadsheet, printed in duplicate on recto and verso. At least 213 copies bound up into a mortgage register; number of cancels undetermined.
TEXT: 49 lines. 365 x 241 mm.
TYPE: BF pica no. 2, long primer no. 2.
PAPER: Imported sheets, at least 15.7 x 12.25 in., marked Pro Patria (94 x 4[20|24|25|25|20]4 mm.)| IV.
LEAF: 15.7 x 12.35 in.
REFERENCES: See notes *sub* Miller 18.
NOTES: Attributed to BF's press on the evidence of the type and cast heading. Franklin cast heading C (letters horizontally hatched; state 2: topmost flourish over the right side of the letter T in "This" nicked at 12 o'clock and slightly flattened; flourish over the letter h in "This" broken at 3 o'clock). Lines 2 and 48 include the decade in their printing of the year, thus: "One Thousand Seven Hundred and Forty [blank]" in the former, "*Anno Domini* 174 [blank]" in the latter. Lines 47-48 read, "Affirm'd at *Philadelphia* the [blank] Day| of [blank] *Anno Domini* 174 [blank]".

One of 213 broadsheets (4 leaves, pp. 1-2, 208-209, 210-211, and 256-7, are loose but present), all printed recto and verso, rebound in the General Loan Office register for 1740-1745 (Philadelphia City Archives spine number 1404). The leaves are paged in contemporary manuscript 1-179, 181-427 (180 mistakenly skipped). The earliest mortgage (p. 1) is dated May 15, 1740; the latest (p. 427) is dated October 24, 1745. The mortgages, however, do not appear on these sequentially numbered pages in as correct a chronological order as they do in some earlier Loan Office registers. If these bonds were printed at the end of 1739, we might tentatively identify them with Charles Brockden's December 10, 1739, credit purchase of "600 records", recorded in BF's Ledger D (see Miller A124 and A127). It is, however, more likely that they were printed early in 1740.
COPIES: Philadelphia, Department of Records, City Archives.

No. 14. Courtesy the American Philosophical Society.

14. 1740 MORTGAGE BONDS FOR THE 1739 RE-EMISSION AND FURTHER STRIKING OF £11,110/5S. SEPARATE SETTING.
PENNSYLVANIA.General Loan Office. This Indenture. Mortgage Bond printed for loans given "pursuant to the Direction of an Act of General Assembly of this Province, made in the *Twelfth* Year of the Reign of His Majesty King *GEORGE the Second*, over *Great-Britain, &c.* entitled, *An ACT for Re-printing, Exchanging and Re-emitting all the Bills of Credit of this Province, and for striking the further Sum of* Eleven Thousand One Hundred and Ten Pounds Five Shillings, *to be emitted upon Loan*".
[No imprint]   [1740]

COLLATION: Folio halfsheet, verso blank.
TEXT: 49 lines. 407 x 240 mm.
TYPE: BF pica no. 2.
PAPER: Imported sheet, at least 22.5 x 16.75 in., Strasbourg lily WR (150 x 7.5[20|27.5|18]9.5 mm.).
LEAF: 16.75 x 11.25 in.
REFERENCES: None found.
NOTES: Attributed to BF's press on the evidence of the type and cast heading. Franklin cast heading C (letters horizontally hatched; state 2: topmost flourish over the right side of the letter T in "This" nicked at 12 o'clock and slightly flattened [defect trimmed away in only located exemplar]; flourish over the letter h in "This" broken at 3 o'clock). Lines 2 and 48 include the decade in their printing of the year, thus: "One Thousand Seven Hundred and Forty [blank]" in the former, "*Anno Domini* 174[blank]" in the latter.

This mortgage bond was printed to be kept by individual mortgagors from the same type page used to print no. 13, with the following modifications: (1) three leaded long primer lines appearing in no. 12 to the left of pica lines 42-44 have been removed; (2) lines 47-48 read, "Affirm'd at *Philadelphia* the [blank]| Day of [blank] *Anno Domini* 174 [blank]"; and (3) lines 22-35 have been leaded.

The PPAmP exemplar (MSS: B/ F85Lf/ no.5/ oversize) was completed in manuscript for Caleb Ransted, mortgagor, on October 15, 1742, and is docketed in manuscript on verso, "Copy of| Caleb Ransted's| M'gage for| £58: 10: 0". (This mortgage is recorded on p. 175 of the General Loan Office register for 1740-45, with notation that on November 28, 1754 the balance due—£34 11s 3d—was paid in full by Samuel Sansom.)
COPY: PPAmP.

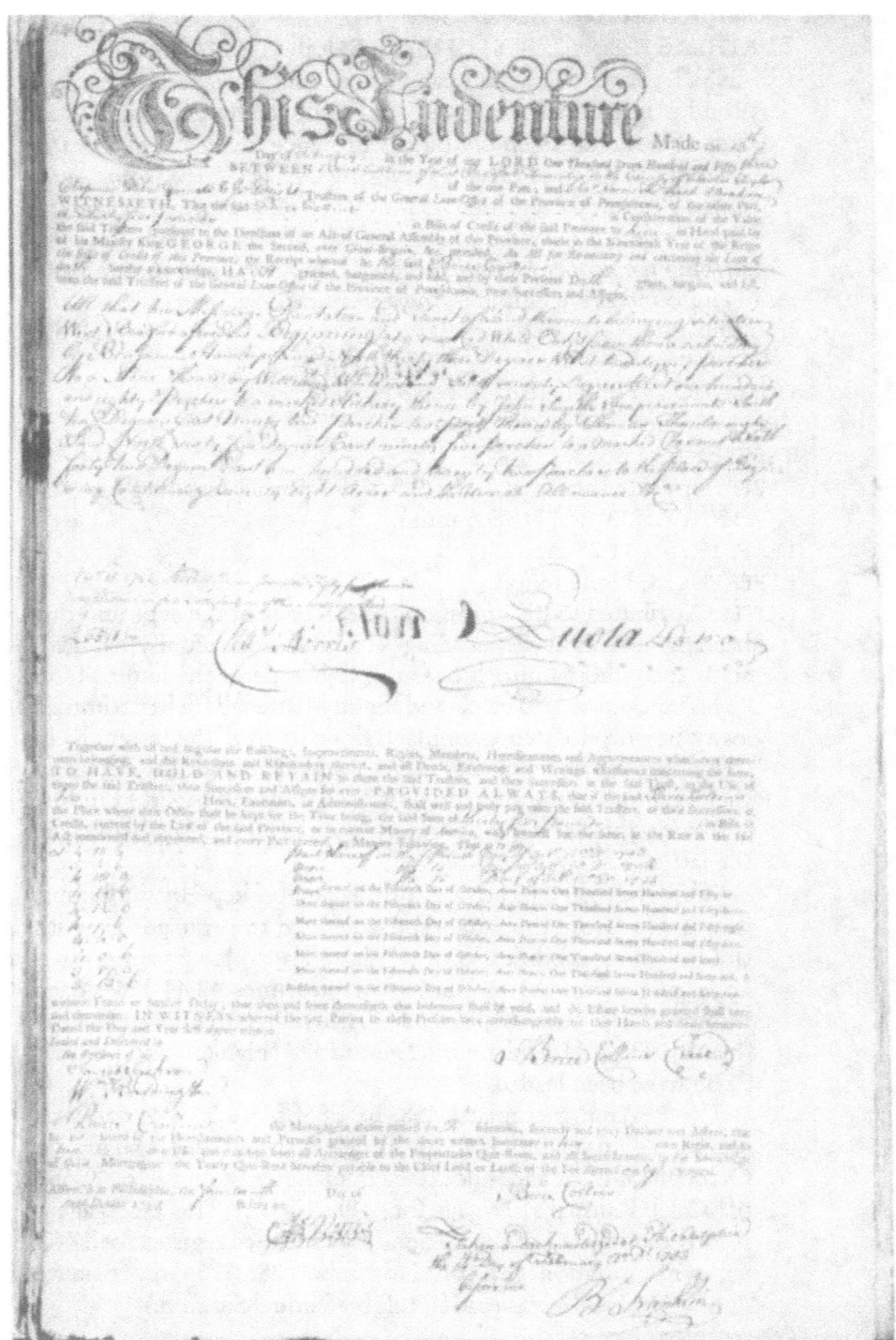

No. 15. Courtesy the City of Philadelphia, Dept. of Records, City Archives.

15. **1752 PENNSYLVANIA GENERAL LOAN OFFICE MORTGAGE REGISTER FOR THE 1746 RE-EMISSION.**
PENNSYLVANIA. General Loan Office. This Indenture. Mortgage Bond printed for loans given "pursuant to the Direction of an Act of General Assembly of this Province, made in the Nineteenth Year of the Reign of his Majesty King GEORGE the Second, over *Great-Britain,* &c. intituled, *An Act for Re-emitting and continuing the Loan of the Bills of Credit of this Province*".
[No imprint] [1752]

COLLATION: Foolscap 2° in fours. 307 leaves, the first 175 paged in contemporary manuscript 1-285, 285-351 (i.e. 350; 285 mistakenly repeated, rectos thence evenly numbered; lacking pp. 1-2, 5-8, 71-72), the remainder unpaged. Signatures and number of cancels undetermined.

TEXT: 38 lines. 388 x 226 mm.

TYPE: BF pica no. 2, long primer no. 2.

PAPER: Imported sheets, at least 21.5 x 16.9 in., marked Strasbourg lily LVG (159 x 5.5[20.5|27.5|22]5.5 mm.) | JW.

LEAF: 16.9 x 10.75 in.

REFERENCES: See notes *sub* Miller 18.

NOTES: Attributed to BF's press on the evidence of the type and cast heading. Franklin cast heading C (letters horizontally hatched; state 2: topmost flourish over the right side of the letter T in "This" slightly flattened at top, nick at 12 o'clock no longer noticeable; flourish over the letter h in "This" broken at 3 o'clock). Lines 2 and 38 both include the decade in their printings of the year, thus: "*One Thousand Seven Hundred and Fifty* [blank]" in the former; "*Anno Domini* 175[blank]" in the latter. The mortgage on p. 3 is dated June 9, 1752; the mortgage on p. 346 is dated August 24, 1756. All rebound in a General Loan Office register for 1752-1756 (spine number 1407).

COPY: Philadelphia, Department of Records, City Archives.

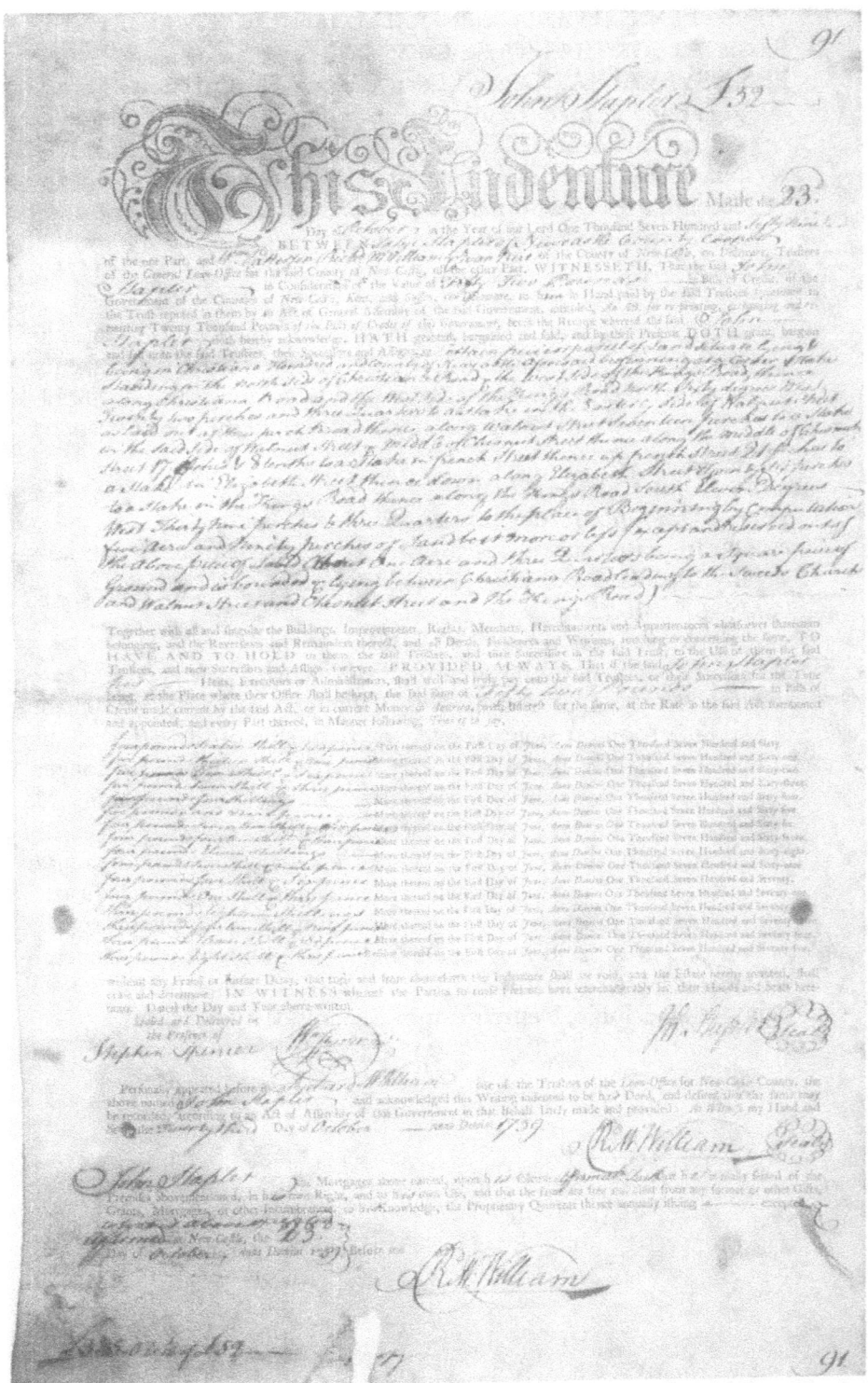

No. 16. Courtesy the Historical Society of Pennsylvania.

Additions to Miller

16. NEW-CASTLE COUNTY (DELAWARE) GENERAL LOAN OFFICE MORTGAGE BOND, 1759.
DELAWARE. New-Castle County General Loan Office. This Indenture. Mortgage Bond printed for loans given "pursuant to the Trust reposed in them [i.e. "[blank] of the County of *New-Castle, on Delaware*, Trustees of the *General Loan-Office* for the said County of *New-Castle*"] by an Act of General Assembly of the said Government, intituled, *An Act for re-printing, exchanging and re-|emitting* Twenty Thousand Pounds *of the Bills of Credit of this Government*, &c."
[No imprint] [1759]

    COLLATION: Folio halfsheet, verso blank.
    TEXT: 49 lines. 369 x 224 mm.
    TYPE: BF pica no. 2, long primer no. 2.
    PAPER: Imported sheet, at least 24.0 x 18.4 in., marked JW.
    LEAF: 18.4 x 12.0 in.
    REFERENCES: See notes *sub* Miller 18.
    NOTES: Attributed to BF's press on the evidence of the type and cast heading. Franklin cast heading C (letters horizontally hatched; state 2: topmost flourish over the right side of the letter T in "This" slightly flattened, nick at 12 o'clock no longer noticeable; flourish over the letter h in "This" broken at 3 o'clock). The act for which these bonds are adapted was passed May 7, 1759 (*Laws of the Government of New-Castle, Kent and Sussex, Upon Delaware*, vol. II, Wilmington: Printed by James Adams, 1763, p. 40).
    DeHi copy 1 (Deeds|1758-1759) completed in manuscript on October 23, 1759, for "John Stapler of Newcastle County cooper." DeHi copy 2 (Deeds|1763) completed in manuscript on June 11, 1763, for "Samuel Armitage of White Clay Creek hundred".
    COPY: DeHi

Appendix:
Index to mortgages recorded in the 1729 Pennsylvania General Loan Office Mortgage register (the Snider volume)

The preceding study has scrutinized the 1729 General Loan Office mortgage register for the light it sheds on the earliest history of Benjamin Franklin and Hugh Meredith's printing office. The Snider volume provides equally useful information for historians of the early Pennsylvania economy, and for prosopographers of colonial Pennsylvania. Some of the data recorded in the Snider volume may prompt re-examination of conclusions reached by historians who necessarily worked without access to the long-lost register. For instance, the Snider volume had not yet been discovered when Mary M. Schweitzer published *Custom and Contract*[108] (a study of the early Pennsylvania economy based on other General Loan Office registers) and Craig Horle and others brought out the first two volumes of *Lawmaking & Legislators in Pennsylvania* (which drew conclusions about the personal indebtedness of its subjects based on the registers then known to be extant and other documents).[109]

The mortgages recorded in the Snider volume account for almost the entire sum lent out under the 1729 "Act for Emitting of Thirty Thousand Pounds in Bills of Credit for the Better Support of Government and the Trade of this Province." The Act required that £26,000 be loaned out (£30,000 less £4,000 set aside in the Act for specified purposes). The Snider volume mortgages total £25,971. The following index gives (a) the name of each mortgagor represented in the Snider volume, (b) the occupation or social status of each mortgagor as added in manuscript to the partially printed mortgage form, (c) each mortgagor's place of residence as added in manuscript to the mortgage form, (d) the amount of paper money loaned to the mortgagor by the General Loan Office, and (e) the Snider volume page number on which each mortgage is recorded.

Addis, John, tanner (Northampton, Bucks) £52. -191

Andrews, George, yeoman (Amity, Philadelphia) £32. -209

---

[108] Mary M. Schweitzer, *Custom and Contract: Household, Government, and the Economy in Colonial Pennsylvania* (New York: Columbia University Press, 1987). See also James M. Duffin, *Guide to the Mortgages of the General Loan Office of the Province of Pennsylvania, 1724-1756* (Philadelphia: City of Philadelphia, Dept. of Records, City Archives, April 1994).

[109] Craig W. Horle, and others, *Lawmaking & Legislators in Pennsylvania: A Biographical Dictionary*, 2 vols. to date (Philadelphia: University of Pennsylvania Press, 1991-).

Mortgagors of 1729

Appleton, Mary, widow (Philadelphia, Philadelphia) £112. -249

Ashburnham, John, yeoman (Mooreland, Philadelphia) £28. -63

Atkinson, William, yeoman (Bristol, Bucks) £48. -195

Baker, Henry, yeoman (Makefield, Bucks) £100. -246

Baker, Samuel, Jr., yeoman (Makefield, Bucks) £152. -245

Baker, Samuel, yeoman (Makefield, Bucks) £300. -244

Ball, John, carpenter (Richland, Bucks) £28. -206

Barlow, Joseph, yeoman (Limerick, Philadelphia) £60. -234

Barns, John, yeoman (Horsham, Philadelphia) £100. -18

Barns, William, blacksmith (Kennet, Chester) £72. -94

Bate, Humphrey, weaver (Concord, Chester) £32. -135

Bayly, Thomas, yeoman (Bucks Co.) £200. -95

Baynes, Thomas, taylor (Philadelphia, Philadelphia; "late of Middletown," Bucks) £52. -120

Beal, Alexander, yeoman (Buckingham, Bucks) £60. -158

Beere, John & Elizabeth, cooper (Philadelphia, Philadelphia) £40. -235

Bennet, Jacob, yeoman (Kennet, Chester) £100. -23

Bennet, William, taylor (Bradford, Chester) £72. -254

Bewley, George, cordwainer (Abington, Philadelphia) £40. - 5

Blaker, Samuel, yeoman (Northampton, Bucks) £56. -202

Bourne, Thomas, merchant (Philadelphia, Philadelphia) £100. -264

Branson, William, shopkeeper (Philadelphia, Philadelphia) £268. -45

Breden, Joseph, weaver (Upper Dublin, Philadelphia) £72. -60

Breintnall, John, whalebone cutter (Philadelphia, Philadelphia) £132. -220

Brinton, William, Jr., — (Thornbury, Chester) £100. -218

Bromfield, Thomas, yeoman (Amity, Philadelphia), £36. -1

Brooks, Edward & Elizabeth, butcher (Philadelphia, Philadelphia) £100. -132

Brown, Peter, shipwright (Philadelphia, Philadelphia) £40. -2

Buffington, Thomas, yeoman (Bradford, Chester) £100. -188

Bye, John, cordwainer (Soulbury, Bucks) £120. -233

Calvert, Daniel, blacksmith (Upper Providence, Chester) £56. -84

Cam, John, stocking weaver (Upper Providence, Chester) £52. -42

Canby, Thomas, Jr., yeoman (Buckingham, Bucks) £100. -193

Carpenter, Samuel, Sr., gentleman (Philadelphia, Philadelphia) £300. -50

Cartlidge, Edmund, — (Conestoga, Lancaster) £188. -112

Carver, William, yeoman (Biberry, Philadelphia) £32. -13

Cawley, John, tanner (Middletown, Bucks) £148. -229

Chamberlin, Jacob, yeoman (Mooreland, Philadelphia) £140. -75

Chancellor, William, sailmaker (Philadelphia, Philadelphia) £260. -126

Charlesworth, Benjamin, yeoman (Whitemarsh, Philadelphia) £52. -58

Charlesworth, Joseph, weaver (Upper Dublin, Philadelphia) £100. -170

Chase, Thomas, merchant (Philadelphia, Philadelphia) £100. -262

Claypoole, George, merchant (Philadelphia, Philadelphia) £300. -106

Cleavor, Derick, weaver (Whitemarsh, Philadelphia) £72. -237

Clifford, Thomas, weaver (Bristol, Bucks) £56. -261

Clymar, Richard, blockmaker (Philadelphia, Philadelphia) £148. -86

Coates, George, sadler (Philadelphia, Philadelphia) £64. -49

Collings, Edward, mason (Cheltenham, Philadelphia) £80. -28

Coppock, Moses, — (Marlborough, Chester) £100. -27

Corker, William, plaisterer (Philadelphia, Philadelphia) £172. -29

Cowpland, Joshua, cordwainer (Chester, Chester) £124. -178

Cox, Thomas, yeoman (Marlborough, Chester) £80. -38

Croasdale, William, yeoman (Newtown, Bucks) £72. -187

Crosley, Charles, weaver (Middletown, Chester) £52. -56

David, Rees, miller (Upper Dublin, Philadelphia) £32. -198

David, Thomas, taylor (Treduffryn [Tredyffrin], Chester) £16. -190

Davis, John, yeoman (Northampton, Bucks) £100. -138

Davis, Sampson & Christina, yeoman (Mooreland, Philadelphia) £200. -4

Davis, William, carpenter (Whitpain, Philadelphia) £60. -255

Dawson, John, feltmaker (Mooreland, Philadelphia) £32. -214

Doane, Daniel, Jr., carpenter (Middletown, Bucks) £32. -119

Doane, Eleazer, yeoman (Middletown, Bucks) £20. -157

Doane, Joseph, carpenter (Wrightstown, Bucks) £20. -136

Dougharty, Edward, cordwainer (Strasburgh, Lancaster) £40. -39

Downey, James, weaver (Makefield, Bucks) £60. -205

Mortgagors of 1729

Downing, Thomas, yeoman (Caln, Chester) £100. -134

Drake, David, yeoman (Wrights Town, Bucks) £148. -61

Drinker, Joseph, carpenter (Philadelphia, Philadelphia) £80. -152

Duer, Joseph, carpenter (Solebury, Bucks) £80. - 7

Dungan, Jeremiah, yeoman (Bucks Co.) £100. -167

Dungan, Thomas, carpenter (Westminster, Bucks) £48. -160

Dungan, William, yeoman (Bristol, Bucks) £48. -257

Durborow, John, scrivener (Philadelphia, Philadelphia) £40. -35

Earl[es], John, yeoman (Westminster, Bucks) £32. -59

Eaton, Joseph, yeoman (Montgomery, Philadelphia) £72. -162

Eavenson, Joseph, yeoman (Thornbury, Chester) £100. -232

Edwards, Joseph, yeoman (Concord, Chester) £140. -147

Edwards, Thomas, yeoman (New Britain, Bucks) £64. -146

Elliot, Andrew, yeoman (Makefield, Bucks) £100. -137

Emlen, George, brewer (Philadelphia, Philadelphia) £200. -192

Emlen, Samuel, sadler (Philadelphia, Philadelphia) £52. -14

Evan, John, yeoman (Uwchland, Chester) £60. -176

Evans, David, vintner (Philadelphia, Philadelphia) £200. -104

Evans, David, yeoman (New Britain, Bucks) £60. -159

Evans, Hugh, yeoman (Merion, Philadelphia) £100. -226

Farmar, Edward, gentleman (Whitemarsh, Philadelphia) £300. -24

Few, James, yeoman (Kennet, Chester) £100. -169

Field, Benjamin, cooper (Middleton, Bucks) £248. -236

Fishbourn, William, Esquire (Philadelphia, Philadelphia) £300. -74

Fisher, William, carpenter (Philadelphia, Philadelphia) £92. -115

Fitzrandolfe, Jonathan, cordwainer (Newtown, Bucks) £160. -21

Flower, John, weaver (Chester Co.) £40. -68

Gatlive, Charles, carpenter (Uwchland, Chester) £60. -64

Gillpin, Joseph, yeoman (Birmingham, Chester) £120. -89

Gissing, David, carpenter (Philadelphia, Philadelphia) £60. -248

Godfrey, Thomas, taylor (Treduffryn [Tredyffrin], Chester) £40. -174

Grandonett, Francis, practitioner of physick (Philadelphia, Philadelphia) £72. -54

Griffith, Morris, yeoman (Willis Town, Chester) £60. -93

Halliday, William, yeoman (New Garden, Chester) £140. -36

Hamer, James, yeoman (Limerick, Philadelphia) £142. -253

Hamilton, James, weaver (Buckingham, Bucks) £116. -8

Harlan, Michael, Jr., yeoman (London Grove, Chester) £60. -110

Harlan, Moses, yeoman (London Grove, Chester) £56. -196

Harmer, William, yeoman (Upper Dublin, Philadelphia) £200. -88

Harris, John, skinner (Gwyneth, Philadelphia) £100. -109

Hasell, Samuel, merchant (Philadelphia, Philadelphia) £140. -9

Hayes, Richard, carpenter (Marlborough, Chester) £60. -53

Helens, Nicholas, yeoman (Bristol, Philadelphia) £188. -66

Helens, Nicholas, yeoman (Bristol, Philadelphia) £92. -65

Hellings, Samuel, yeoman (Bristol, Philadelphia) £120. -194

Henry, David, yeoman (Manatawny, Philadelphia) £76. -57

Hewes, Moses, taylor (Philadelphia, Philadelphia) £52. -221

Hewes, William, mason (Chichester, Chester) £132. -207

Hibbert, Aaron, yeoman (Blockley, Philadelphia) £88. -43

Hibbs, William, yeoman (Northampton, Bucks) £32. -99

Hill, William, fuller (Middletown, Chester) £64. -79

Hillborn, John, yeoman (New Town, Bucks) £100. -155

Hillborn, Thomas, yeoman (New Town, Bucks) £48. -154

Hilldegrass, Michael, potter (Philadelphia, Philadelphia) £80. -141

Holt, Samuel, cooper (Philadelphia, Philadelphia) £36. -19

Hough, Francis, sawyer (Buckingham, Bucks) £64. -69

Hough, John, yeoman (Solebury, Bucks) £88. -71

Houlton, Nathaniel, sawyer (New Garden, Chester) £92. -182

Howell, Thomas, yeoman (Northampton, Bucks) yeoman £40. -98

Hubbs, Charles, Sr., yeoman (Upper Dublin, Philadelphia) £200. -90

Huddleston, William, cordwainer (Middletown, Bucks) £52. -260

Hughes, Evan, yeoman (East Town, Chester) £96. -128

Hughes, Morgan, yeoman (Easttown, Chester) £48. -10

Hulings, Michael, shipwright (Philadelphia, Philadelphia) £72. -144

Huling[s], Marcus, yeoman (Amity, Philadelphia) £52. -121

Mortgagors of 1729

Hulme, George, yeoman (Middletown, Bucks) £132. -228

Hutton, John, taylor (New Garden, Chester) £48. -172

James, Mordecai, sadler (Goshen, Chester) £60. -180

James, Thomas, yeoman (Willis-town, Chester) £88. -30

Janney, Thomas, carpenter (Makefield, Chester) £100 -123

Jemison, Alexander, yeoman (Northhampton, Bucks) £88. -185

Jemison, Henry, yeoman (Southampton, Bucks) £80. -183

Jemison, Robert, yeoman (Northampton, Bucks) £88. -184

Jenkins, Phineas, — (Abington, Philadelphia) £52. -17

Jennings, Benjamin, yeoman (Solebury, Bucks) £60. -148

Johnson, Jacob, yeoman (Newtown, Bucks) £80. -165

Johnson, John, yeoman (Newtown, Bucks) £64. -166

Jonason, Peter, yeoman (Kingsessing, Philadelphia) £100. -96

Jones, David, yeoman (New Brittain, Bucks) £60. -118

Jones, Jonas, cordwainer (Kingsessing, Philadelphia) £68. -20

Jones, Malachi, yeoman (Abington, Philadelphia) £100. -108

Kastner, George, yeoman (Whitpain, Philadelphia) £92. -114

Kelly, Patrick, yeoman (Mooreland, Philadelphia) £52. -100

Kirkbride, Joseph, gentleman (Bucks Co.) £300. -72

Kirkbride, Mahlon, yeoman (Makefield, Bucks) £220. -70

Lancaster, Thomas, yeoman (Bucks Co.) £40. -77

Large, John, taylor (Bristol, Bucks) £52. -142

Leacock, John, merchant (Philadelphia, Philadelphia) £100. -15

Leech, Thomas, merchant (Philadelphia, Philadelphia) £100. -143

Lewis, George, yeoman (Charles town, Chester) £48. -231

Lewis, Joseph, yeoman (Haverford, Chester) £48. -151

Lewis, Stephen, yeoman (Charlestown, Chester) £52. -203

Lightfoot, Michael, weaver (Newgarden, Chester) £80. -82

Llewelyn, David, yeoman (Haverford, Chester) £100. -139

Lloyd, Peter, merchant (Philadelphia, Philadelphia) £300. -105

Lloyd, Thomas, yeoman (Mooreland, Philadelphia) £56. -78

Lord, Theodorus, merchant (Passyunck, Philadelphia) £100 -3

MacVeagh, Edmund, Jr., carpenter (Lower Dublin, Philadelphia) £64. -16
Maddock, Mordecai, yeoman (Springfield, Chester) £100. -51
Matthew, Simon, millwright (New Britain, Bucks) £160. -150
Maulsby, David, blacksmith (Mooreland, Philadelphia) £124. -263
Maybury, Thomas, blacksmith (Newtown, Bucks) £48. -259
McVeagh, Jeremiah, yeoman (Abington, Philadelphia) £32. -117
Melchior, William, blacksmith (Upper Dublin, Philadelphia) £32. -199
Meredith, Simon, yeoman (Chester Co.) £132. -243
Milnor, John, yeoman (Makefield, Bucks) £200. -175
Mitchell, George, yeoman (Wrights Town, Bucks) £52. -219
Montgomery, John, yeoman (Makefield, Bucks) £72. -216
Moore, Thomas, yeoman (Caln, Chester) £300. -204
Morgan, Evan, taylor (Philadelphia, Philadelphia) £180. -111
Morris, Anthony, brewer (Philadelphia, Philadelphia) £300. -250
Morris, Thomas, yeoman (Hilltown, Bucks) £72. -156
Morris, William, yeoman (Willis Town, Chester) £100. -85
Nelson, Henry, yeoman (Middletown, Bucks) £200. -102
Newberry, Richard, yeoman (Bristol, Philadelphia) £100. -40
Ogilby, John, yeoman (Biberry, Philadelphia) £80. -181
Owen, John, carpenter (Chester, Chester) £100. -140
Owen, William, joiner (Marple, Chester) £60. -130
Parry or Perry, Thomas, yeoman (Mooreland, Philadelphia) £52. -213
Parry, David, yeoman (Cheltenham, Philadelphia) £84. -37
Parsons, William, cordwaineer (Philadelphia, Philadelphia) £44. -76
Penquite, Nicholas, yeoman (Northampton, Bucks) £52. -97
Peters, Rice, shopkeeper (Philadelphia, Philadelphia) £80. -197
Peters, Thomas, shopkeeper (Philadelphia, Philadelphia) £124. -12
Petty, John, merchant (Philadelphia, Philadelphia) £200. -222
Phillips, David, yeoman (Limerick, Philadelphia) £60. -210
Pile, William, Jr., yeoman (Birmingham, Chester) £52. -177
Poole, Nathaniel & Ann, shipwright (Philadelphia, Philadelphia) £176. -48
Poole, Nathaniel, shipwright (Philadelphia, Philadelphia) £100. -47
Potts, David, yeoman (Bristol, Philadelphia) £48. -91

Mortgagors of 1729

Powell, Samuel, carpenter (Philadelphia, Philadelphia) £200. -208

Powell, Samuel, Jr., merchant (Philadelphia, Philadelphia) £72. -153

Powell, William, cooper (Philadelphia, Philadelphia) £52. -62

Preston, Samuel, Esqr. (Passyunk, Philadelphia) £132. -241

Preston, Samuel, Esqr. (Passyunk, Philadelphia) £168. -242

Pugh, Thomas, taylor (Middletown, Bucks) £80. -227

Rakestraw, William, carter (Philadelphia, Philadelphia) £60. -131

Rawle, Joseph, cooper (Philadelphia, Philadelphia) £94. -26

Read, Sarah, widow (Philadelphia, Philadelphia) £140. -225

Reece, Thomas, yeoman (Newtown, Chester) £100. -149

Reese, Thomas, yeoman (New Brittain, Bucks) £72. -211

Richard, William, yeoman (Amity, Philadelphia) £48. -129

Richardson, John, yeoman (Bristol, Philadelphia) £132. -44

Roberts, Ann, widow (Nantwell, Chester) £300. -238

Rodes, Richard, yeoman (Passyunk, Philadelphia) £48. -127

Roger, Owen, miller (Treduffryn [Tredyffrin], Chester) £56. -173

Roman, Jacob, yeoman (Chester, Chester) £52. -25

Salkeld, John, yeoman (Chester, Chester) £200. -164

Sanders, Robert, yeoman (Wrightstown, Bucks) £40. -6

Sharman, Robert, yeoman (Marlborough, Chester) £148. -161

Sharples, Joseph, yeoman (Middletown, Chester) £160. -80

Sharswood, George, cordwainer (Philadelphia, Philadelphia) £40. -217

Shewell, Robert, cooper (Middletown, Bucks) £100. -252

Shewell, Walter, yeoman (New Britain, Bucks) £100. -251

Sill, James, sawyer (Edgmond, Chester) £52. -101

Skelton, John, yeoman (Buckingham, Bucks) £32. -258

Smith, Thomas, —(Windy Buch, Bucks) £36. -11

Smith, William, Jr., yeoman (Wrightstown, Bucks) £48. -116

Sober, Thomas, merchant (Philadelphia, Philadelphia) £200. -92

Stackhouse, Thomas, yeoman (Middletown, Bucks) £200. -41

Stanaland, Thomas, yeoman (Bucks Co.) £52. -223

Stevans, Evan, yeoman (New Britain, Bucks) £200. -247

Stevens, Mary, widow (Birmingham, Chester) £36. -215

Thomas, John, yeoman (Whitpain, Philadelphia) £100. -256

Thomas, Richard, yeoman (Horsham, Philadelphia) £68. -83

Thomason, Joshua, yeoman (Ridley, Chester) £72. -189

Thompson, Christopher, bricklayer (Philadelphia, Philadelphia) £100. -163

Townsend, James, yeoman (Birmingham, Chester) £124. -124

Townsend, Joseph, weaver (Bradford, Chester) £200. -22

Tucker, Joseph, carpenter (Cheltenham, Philadelphia) £48. -52

Tunes, Anthony, weaver (Germantown, Philadelphia) £100. -81

Turner, Charles, cordwainer (Birmingham, Chester) £68. -125

Underwood, John, carpenter (Bristol, Bucks) £40. -87

Vandegrift, Jacob, yeoman (Bensalen, Bucks) £52. -230

Vanhorne, Peter Barnson, yeoman (Middletown, Bucks) £248. -107

Vaughan, John, carpenter (Uwchland, Chester) £100. -32

Vernon, Isaac, yeoman (Goshen, Chester) £100. -240

Wade, John, yeoman (Chester, Chester) £148. -168

Waever, Richard, carpenter (Chester, Chester) £100. -145

Walmsley, Henry & Mary, yeoman (Bucks Co.) £76. -67

Ward, John, yeoman (Whitpain, Philadelphia) £48. -133

Warder, Richard, gentleman (Philadelphia, Philadelphia) £100. -200

Warder, Richard, gentleman (Philadelphia, Philadelphia) £64. -201

Warder, Solomon, yeoman (Falls, Bucks) £52. -239

Waring, John, yeoman (Amity, Philadelphia) £40. -33

Warner, Joseph, yeoman (Wrightstown, Bucks) £80. -113

Watson, Nathan, cordwainer (Bristol, Bucks) £100. -73

Webb, Daniel, wheelwright (Kennet, Chester) £80. -186

Whiting, James, yeoman (Southhampton, Bucks) £44. -46

Williams, Nicholas, rug weaver (Buckingham, Bucks) £32. -212

Williamson, Thomas, yeoman (Edgmont, Chester) £100. -179

Wood, Abraham, mason (Makefield, Bucks) £100. -103

Wood, Josiah, carpenter (Cheltenham, Philadelphia) £32. -55

Wood, Josiah, yeoman (Falls township, Bucks) £80. -34

Worthington, Daniel, yeoman (Shackamaxon, Philadelphia) £100. -31

Mortgagors of 1729

Wright, Jacob, yeoman (Willis Town, Chester) £100. -224
Yarnall, John, yeoman (Edgmont, Chester) £100. -171
Yeardley, Thomas, cooper (Makefield, Bucks) £300. -122

INDEX

The names of mortgagors whose mortgages are recorded in the 1729 Register are given in the Appendix on pp. 78-87 and are not redundantly indexed here. BF = Benjamin Franklin.

Advertisements, Franklin & Meredith's, for their publications, 11- 12, 12n34, 12n38, 24, 26

Africans & African-Americans, Franklin & Meredith print Ralph Sandiford's tract opposing the enslavement of, 7-8

American Weekly Mercury (newspaper printed by Andrew Bradford), 10n32, 11

Armitage, Samuel, 1763 Delaware mortgagor, 77

bookbinding, fig. A, 1, 1n1, 15, 16, 22, 22n67, 39

Bradford, Andrew, printer, 1, 2, 4, 8, 10-11, 20, 24, 25n77, 32; prints Pennsylvania paper money in 1723, 1726, and1729, 14 15; prints New Jersey loan office registers in 1724, 15n50, 16, 18-19 (figs. C & D); quality of his printing, 10-11, 18 (fig. C), 19 (fig. D), 20, 24, 25

Bradford, William, printer, 4

Bradford, William, Jr., printer, 25n77, 65

Breintnall, Joseph, scrivener & friend of BF, assists Franklin & Meredith, 7, 23, 24, 29, 33, 36

Brief Examination of the Practice of the Times (Sandiford), 7 8

Brockden, Charles, clerk of the Pennsylvania General Loan office, 20, 27, 71

Carpenter, Samuel, trustee of Pennsylvania General Loan Office, 34

Coleman, William, loans money to BF, 29

Davies, William, bookbinder, 1, 39

Dawson, John, 1734 mortgagor, 53

Delaware: paper money, printed by Franklin & Meredith in 1729, 20, 25, 26; mortgage bonds, printed by Franklin & Meredith, 26, 29n86, 45-47, printed by Franklin & Hall, 76, 77

Edgell, Simon, rents building to Franklin & Meredith, 4

Fishbourn, William, trustee of Pennsylvania General Loan Office, 34, 38-39; embezzles Loan Office money, 21n63, 38; stages burglary, 38

Franklin, Benjamin: works for Samuel Keimer, 5; quits working for Keimer, 4, 7; obtains Breintnall's help to secure printing of 44½ sheets of Keimer s edition of Sewel's *History of the Quakers*, 7; petitions Pennsylvania Assembly to print for it, 8; reads in economics, 9; leads Junto discussion of paper money, 10; reprints Andrew Bradford's printing of the Assembly's address to Gov. Gordon, 10-11; prints Delaware paper money in 1729, 20, 26; terminates partnership with Meredith, 29, 30; attitude toward taxation, 32; counter-factual storytelling, 30-31; cultivation of accessible prose style, 32; devotion to community, 31-32; program for early retirement from manual labor, 31, cf. 7; originality, 32-33; quality of his memory, 30-31. Printing by: high quality of, 19 (fig. E), 24, 24n75,

Index

38; compared to Andrew Bradford's 10, 25; care taken to insure high quality of, 10, 13, 28; textual errors in, 45, 63, 67, 69, cf. 28-29. Writings: account books, 23n68; *Autobiography*, 2, 7, 8, 9, 10, 13, 14n42, 20, 21, 23, 24, 25, 28, 30; *Father Abraham's speech*, 32; *A Modest Inquiry into the Nature and Necessity of a Paper-Currency*, 2, 11 12, 13, 22, 25, 30, 32; petition to the Pennsylvania Assembly, 8, 9; *Pennsylvania Gazette*, 12n38, 26, 62; *Poor Richard*, 31, 32; *Way to Wealth*, 32.

Franklin, James, printer, brother of BY, 5n9, 12

Gender-neutral text for partially printed legal forms, 28-29; see also Women as mortgagors

Godfrey, Thomas, publisher of Franklin & Meredith's 1729 printing of Watts's *Psalms of David*, 13; author of almanac for 1730, 26

Gordon, Patrick, governor of Pennsylvania, 2, 9, 11, 13, 26

Grace, Robert, loans money to BF, 29

Hamilton, James, 1740 mortgagor, 67
Hamilton, James, patron of BF, 20, 25, 33

Handwritten documents: see Writing with pen & ink

Harry, David, printer, 26, 33n97

Hayes, Richard, not approved as a Pennsylvania General Loan Office trustee, 38 39

History of the Quakers (Sewel), 6-7, 8, 12

Horle, Craig W., historian, 78

Hughes, Matthew, dedicatee of *Brief Examination* (Sandiford), 8

Jordan, Mary & Robert, 1737 mortgagors, 59; 1740 mortgagors, 65, 67

Junto (Philadelphia self-improvement society), 7, 10, 24n74, 26

Keimer. Samuel, printer, 4, 5, 6-7, 12, 33m97; prints New Jersey paper money with BF's assistance, 15n50; sells printing office to David Harry, 26

Kinsey, John, trustee of Pennsylvania General Loan Office, embezzles Loan Office money, 21n63

Langhorne, Jeremiah, trustee of Pennsylvania General Loan Office, 34

Lawmaking & Legislators in Pennsylvania; A Biographical Dictionary Horle and others), 2, 78

Lemay, J.A. Leo, historian, 7, 8, 10

Meredith, Hugh, 1 et passim; works for Samuel Keimer, 5; quits working for Keimer, 4, 7; vices, 4, 30; partnership with BF ends, 29, 30; absence from known historical sources generated after 1749, 30n91

Meredith, John, *Short Discourse, Proving that the Jewish or Seventh-Day Sabbath Is Abrogated and Repealed*, 26

Miller, C. William, historian, 1, 2, 3, 40, 41

New Jersey, loan office registers, printed by Andrew Bradford, 15n50, 16, 18 20; printed by BF, 56, 57

Newlin, Nathaniel, trustee of Pennsylvania General Loan Office, 2, 34, 37, 38, 49

paper, use of royal or large required by Pennsylvania Assembly, 15, 16; efficient use of, 25; see also Watermarks

paper money, printing of, 14-15, 20, 26

Penn family, 5, 9

Pennsylvania Assembly, 2, 6, 8, 9, 10, 13, 14, 15, 21, 25, 26, 30, 31, 38; legislated emissions of paper money: 1723 (first), 5 6, 15, 16; 1723 (second), 6, 16; 1726, 6, 16, 27, 28, 34; 1729, 13, 14, 15, 27, 34, 37, 38

Pennsylvania Gazette (newspaper printed by Franklin & Meredith), 12n38, 26, 62

Pennsylvania General Loan office, 1, 6,

14, 15, 20, 21, 25, 26, 34; establishment of, 5; see also Scriveners.
Philadelphia Yearly Meeting (Society of Friends), 6-7
Psalms of David (Watts), 12, 13, 13n39

Ransted, Caleb, 1742 mortgagor, 73
Rawle, Francis, *Some Remedies Proposed, for the Restoring the Sunk Credit of the Province of Pennsylvania*, 10n29, 33
Read, Charles, trustee of Pennsylvania General Loan Office, disappearance of his handwritten name from mortgages, and subsequent death of, 62
Robin Hood's Songs, 12n38

Sandiford, Ralph, *A Brief Examination of the Practice of the Times*, 7-8
Schweitzer, Mary M., historian, 78
Scriveners, 7, 20, 44; see also Writing with pen & ink
Scull, Nicholas, friend of Franklin, 24
sex-neutral printing, 28-29
Sewel, Samuel, *History of the Quakers*, 6-7, 8, 12
Short Discourse, Proving that the Jewish or Seventh-Day Sabbath Is Abrogated and Repealed (Meredith), 26
slavery in colonial America, 7-8
Snider, Jay, book collector, I
Some Remedies Proposed, for the Restoring the Sunk Credit of the Province of Pennsylvania (Rawle), 10n29, 33
South Sea Company (London), collapse of its stock, 5, 5n12, 6, 33
Spirit's Teaching Man's Sure Guide (Woolverton), 26
Stamp Act (1765), colonial opposition to, 32
Stapler, John, 1759 Delaware mortgagor, 77
Starr, Thomas, historian, 27n83
Stevenson, Allan, historian, 41

taxation, BF's attitude towards, 32
Taylor, Philip, trustee of Pennsylvania General Loan Office, 2, 34, 37, 38, 49, 51

type: Andrew Bradford's, 10-11;
  BF's pica no. 1: 1, 43, 45, 49, 51, 53, 55, 59, 61;
  BF's pica no. 2: 63, 67, 69, 71, 73, 75, 77;
  BF's long primer no. 1; 57;
  BF's long primer no. 2: 71, 75, 77;
  BF's cast heading A; 35, 36, 43, 49, 51, 53;
  BF's cast heading B: 45;
  BF's cast heading C: 55, 57, 59, 61, 63, 67, 69, 71, 73, 75, 77

Universal Instructor in all Arts and Sciences: and Pennsylvania Gazette (newspaper printed by Keimer), 25-26

Walton, Joshua, 1734 mortgagor, 55
Watermarks:
  Arms of Amsterdam | crown GAS, 61;
  Arms of Amsterdam | H, 57;
  Arms of Amsterdam |ANDEL (?), 61;
  Arms of Amsterdam |ML, 53, 55;
  JW, 7;
  Pro Patria | crown GR, 59;
  Pro Patria |, IV, 69, 71;
  Strasbourg bend | IV (aka Strasbourg bend and lily-IV), 1, 43, 45, 49, 51, 67;
  Strasbourg lily LVG | IV, 63;
  Strasbourg lily LVG | JW, 75;
  Strasbourg lily WR, 63
Watts, Isaac, *Psalms of David*, 12, 13
Wolf, Clarence, antiquarian book dealer, I
Women as mortgagors, 28, 29, 28n85, 59, 65, 79, 80, 84, 85, 86
Woolverton, Charles, *The Spirit's Teaching Man's Sure Guide*, 26
Wright, Esmond, historian, 31
Writing with pen & ink, 16, 17 (fig. B), 20, 25, 27, 39; customary mingling of with letterpress printing, 1, 14-15, 27, 27n83, 28, 29, 34n99, 39, and all the illustrations in Section III.

www.ingramcontent.com/pod-product-compliance
Lightning Source LLC
Chambersburg PA
CBHW080801020526
44114CB00035B/6